Look, Dude, I Can Cook!

Amy Madden

Look, Dude, I Can Cook!

FOUR YEARS OF COLLEGE COOKING MADE EASY

HOLY COW!!
REAL FOOD!!!

SYREN BOOK COMPANY
MINNEAPOLIS

Published by
Syren Book Company
5120 Cedar Lake Road
Minneapolis, MN 55416
763-398-0030
www.syrenbooks.com

Printed in the United States of America on acid-free paper

ISBN 978-0-929636-78-8

LCCN 2007927184

Cover design by Kyle G. Hunter
Interior text design by Wendy Holdman
Photos by Woodie Williams
Drawings by Megan Thorson

To order additional copies of this book, please go to www.itascabooks.com.

With love, to all the students in my life:

Megan, Mark, Scott, Alex, and Zack

Contents

Acknowledgments

*Thanks to all of the kids who prompted me to write this book and to the people
who gave me their encouragement and support:*

Megan for her creative input and imaginative cartoons.

Zack for his witty contributions.

Mark for rounding up his friends and for always being happy to offer his precious time.

Scott and Alex for their encouragement and suggestions.

Liz for being my sounding board and never-ending support.

Kimberly Kennedy, whose words gave me the epiphany to write this book.

My friends Carmen, Rhonda, and Avid, whose faith in me never falters.

Gary for his love and support.

Introduction

Just because you're off to college doesn't mean you have to do without those home-cooked meals you crave. A taste of home is never far away if you can read, follow instructions, and have a true desire to create a meal that would make Mom and Dad and especially yourself proud. Assuming the first two abilities (reading and following instructions) are among the reasons you're in college, the only thing left is the desire to make some good food while you're there. *Look, Dude, I Can Cook!* will provide you with the know-how to prepare a range of dishes, from basic to easy gourmet. Although most of the recipes are very healthy, there are some low-fat variations for those who are weight conscious, as well as suggestions for mixing it up a bit or making it easier and/or saving you a few dollars.

The recipes that follow are divided into four chapters: Freshman, Sophomore, Junior, and Senior, and run the gamut of simple to easy going gourmet, getting progressively more challenging as the years go on. Students can skip a year if they're feeling adventurous or return to a year that holds good memories. Whether you're a freshasaurus, a bag monster, a hip heroine, zombied, preparing for an antler festival, or hooking up with that special someone, there's a recipe for every occasion. On football Saturdays, if you want to do a little frontloading, check out the Tailgating section in the back of the book to plan your menu. You'll also find in the back a list of cooking utensils and pantry items you'll need for college, as well as a glossary of cooking terms.

I got the idea for writing this cookbook when my son, Mark, went off to college. He frequently called me for recipes, and then one day he asked me to just write some down so that he wouldn't have to keep calling me. My daughter Megan, who was already in her third year of college and had had some training in the kitchen, was better equipped, but she also called me for cooking advice and some of my special recipes. That's when I decided to write *Look, Dude, I Can Cook!* Because of my years as a caterer and baker, I had an overwhelming supply of recipes in my head, and this book contains many of my favorites and my kids' favorites. *Look, Dude, I Can Cook!* is a progressive cookbook, and since many of you college kids seem to have a language of your own, I thought it might be fun to incorporate some of the slang used at colleges around the country. For those who have never heard the words used here, you can check out the introductions to the chapters or the glossary in the back of the book, which has many more words and phrases. I found many of the terms to be quite amusing, even if they aren't frequently used.

This cookbook contains over one hundred recipes designed to help every college student create meals that are bound to satisfy you and your college mates. Take the shortcut or use a variation if you want to keep it simple or mix it up. *Look, Dude, I Can Cook!* is full of recipes you can continue to use well after graduation. Enjoy!

Getting Frosh: Your Freshman Year

Let's forget about the so-called Freshman 15. In this chapter you'll find recipes that are healthy, easy to prepare, and guaranteed to keep you from using *FLWs* such as, "I'll buy my roommate a new bag of chips tomorrow . . . he [or she] won't notice." There has been many a roommate brawl over an empty bag of Ruffles and the crusted remnants of French dip. You'll have fond memories of those FLWs, but so will your waistline.

These recipes will keep you from falling victim to the Freshman 15 rite of passage so that you don't end up in the *quack shack* later in life. Your first year of college is a good time to prove to yourself that you don't need Mom looking over your shoulder telling you what you should eat and you don't have to be an *Alpha Greek* to prepare your own food.

Lesson Plan: Walk around and get a feel for your surroundings. Find out where the nearest grocery store and farmers' market are located. Get organized and make a list before you go to the store. This will help you stay on a budget and prevent you from overspending.

Alpha Greek: the male or female who rules the school's Greek system—or thinks they do.

FLWs: famous last words.

Quack shack: college health facility.

Fruit and Honey Smoothies

The good thing about smoothies is that you can combine any of your favorite fruits, juices, and yogurts and mix them up. This is a filling, healthy snack.

1 banana

5 strawberries

1 cup pineapple chunks

¾ cup orange or milk

1 teaspoon vanilla (optional)

1 tablespoon honey

1½ cup ice cubes

Break banana into pieces and put in blender. Trim stems and leaves from strawberries and place in blender. Add pineapple, orange juice or milk, vanilla, honey, and ice. Blend until smooth. Serves 2.

Variation: Add two heaping teaspoons of your favorite protein powder. Mix it up with your favorite fruits—have fun.

Biscuits with Grandma's Gravy

This is an easy recipe that even works for a light Sunday supper.

1 tube Pillsbury's Grand Flaky Biscuits

4 slices crispy bacon (optional)

4 level tablespoons butter

4 level tablespoons flour

2 cups milk

salt and pepper to taste

Cook biscuits according to package instructions and set aside.

Place bacon on plate and cover with a paper towel. Microwave for 2 minutes. Discard the paper towel and place a new paper towel over bacon and microwave another 2 minutes or until bacon is crispy. Transfer to a plate covered with a paper towel and set aside. When cool, break bacon into bits.

Heat butter in a small saucepan over medium heat. When the butter is bubbling (be careful not to let it turn brown), add the flour and stir with a wire whisk to make a nice thick paste. Slowly, adding a little at a time, whisk in the milk. Continue stirring until gravy thickens (about 5 minutes). Season with salt and pepper. To serve, take two biscuits and cut each one in half and place on a plate. Pour ½ cup of gravy over biscuits and sprinkle with bacon bits. Serves 4.

Low-fat variation: Substitute low-fat biscuits for Pillsbury's Grand Flaky Biscuits; turkey bacon for regular bacon; light margarine for butter; skim milk for whole milk.

Vanilla French Toast

This is the easiest way to make French toast just like Mom's.

2 eggs

¼ cup milk

1 teaspoon vanilla

¼ teaspoon cinnamon

2 tablespoons butter

4 slices bread—whole wheat or white

maple syrup or powdered sugar

Beat eggs with milk. Add the vanilla and cinnamon, and mix well. Heat 1 tablespoon butter in a nonstick skillet over medium heat; dip 2 bread slices in the egg mixture and put in skillet. Brown one side and then flip and brown the other side. Repeat with remaining butter and bread slices. Serve with maple syrup or powdered sugar. Serves 2.

Low-fat variation: Substitute egg whites for eggs; skim milk for whole milk; light margarine for butter; any variety of light syrup.

Soups, Salads, and Starters

As You Like It—Mexican Salsa

What's good about this recipe is that you can serve it hot or cold. So if you don't have access to a microwave or cooktop, you can just as easily make the cold version.

1 clove garlic, minced

½ onion, minced

4 medium tomatoes, chopped

minced jalapeño pepper to taste
   (If you like it hot, add a whole pepper; otherwise, start with a small amount and add to reach your preferred degree of hotness. Omitting the seeds will reduce the level of hotness considerably. Simply cut pepper in half and carefully scrape out the seeds with a knife and discard. Be careful not to touch the seeds as some people have an allergic reaction to them. Never rub your eyes after handling hot peppers.)

½ teaspoon cumin

½ cup chopped fresh cilantro

This salsa can be served hot or cold. For cold, combine all ingredients and serve. For hot, heat 2 tablespoons olive oil in small skillet and sauté garlic and onion until soft. Add the tomatoes and jalapeño pepper and cook until most of the liquid from the tomatoes has evaporated. Stir in cumin and cilantro and serve with tortilla chips.

Variation: For fresh tomatoes, substitute one 16-ounce can diced tomatoes. To make in the microwave, put 1 tablespoon olive oil, onion, and garlic in a microwavable dish, cook on high for about 3–4 minutes. Then add tomatoes, cumin, and jalapeño, and cook for another 4–5 minutes. Take out and add the chopped cilantro.

Creamy Chili con Queso

If you like restaurant-style chili con queso, this is the ticket.

8 ounces sliced American cheese, torn into pieces

8 ounces shredded medium cheddar cheese

1 10-ounce can diced tomatoes with green chilies, drained well

¼ cup milk

minced jalapeño pepper to taste
(If you like it hot, add a whole pepper; otherwise, start with a small amount and add to reach your preferred degree of hotness. Omitting the seeds will reduce the level of hotness considerably. Simply cut pepper in half and carefully scrape out the seeds with a knife and discard. Be careful not to touch the seeds as some people have an allergic reaction to them. Never rub your eyes after handling hot peppers.)

Place all ingredients in a medium saucepan. Heat over low heat, stirring frequently to prevent cheese from sticking, until the cheese is melted to a smooth consistency. Serve with tortilla chips.

Variation: Sauté ½ cup of onion and 1 minced clove garlic in 1 tablespoon butter. Add the tomatoes, cheeses, and milk. Stir over low heat until cheese melts to a smooth consistency.

Pan con Tomate

This is the Spanish version of bruchetta, but it's easier and very delicious.

ciabatta bread or crusty French bread

1 clove garlic, unpeeled and cut in half

1 tomato, sliced in half

olive oil for drizzling

salt to taste

Cut bread into 2 thick slices. If using French bread, cut a long section and then slice in half. Toast the bread in a toaster or toaster oven. When bread is nicely browned, remove and place on a plate. Using one of the garlic clove halves, gently rub the toasted bread. (The harder you rub, the stronger the garlic flavor.) Then rub one of the tomato halves over the bread, squeezing slightly to extract some of the pulp. Drizzle with olive oil and sprinkle with salt. Repeat with second slice and enjoy immediately.

Chopped Salad Your Way

Whether you're in a dorm or not, this versatile recipe can be made anywhere.

1 bag of your favorite mixed lettuce, chopped (and washed)

3 stalks celery, chopped

2 cooked chicken breasts, chopped (shortcut: use breast meat from a rotisserie chicken)

1 cup chopped tomatoes

1 cucumber, chopped

1 carrot, chopped

1 red bell pepper, chopped

1 cup of your favorite cheese (blue cheese and feta cheese work well)

Chop all ingredients and put in a bowl. Toss with vinaigrette dressing or use your favorite creamy dressing. Serves 2–4.

Vinaigrette Dressing

2 tablespoons red wine vinegar

½ level teaspoon sugar

1 level teaspoon Dijon mustard

Salt and pepper to taste

5 tablespoons olive oil

Whisk together the vinegar, sugar, mustard, salt, and pepper. Add the olive oil and whisk until mixture is blended.

Vegetarian variation: Omit the chicken and add chickpeas or tofu and any of your favorite vegetables.

Healthy Fruit Salad

You can mix it up with this recipe, adding or substituting any of your favorite fruits, nuts, and yogurt.

1 apple, peeled, cored, and diced

1 cup pineapple chunks

1 banana, peeled and diced

1 cup strawberries, cleaned and quartered

1½ cups vanilla yogurt

¼ level teaspoon cinnamon

½ level cup chopped pecans

Place the fruit in a bowl and toss. Mix together the yogurt and cinnamon and pour over fruit and mix. Add nuts and mix well. Sprinkle top with cinnamon. Serves 2.

The Lighter Side

Turkey Wraps

These wraps can be served hot or cold. If you don't have a cooktop, use a microwave and follow the variation method.

2 large (about 11 inches in diameter) white, whole wheat, or flavored wraps

2 tablespoons chopped cilantro

2 tablespoons mayonnaise

½ pound sliced smoked or regular turkey breast

¼ pound thinly sliced Swiss cheese or your favorite cheese

1 small jar pimientos, drained

⅔ cup chopped lettuce

½ cup chopped purple onion (optional)

Lay the wraps flat. Mix together the mayonnaise and cilantro. Spread each wrap with the cilantro-mayonnaise mixture without going all the way to the edge; then layer with a couple of slices of turkey, cheese, a tablespoon of pimientos, lettuce, and onion. Fold sides of tortilla over ends of filling and roll up burrito-style, enclosing filling completely. Cut in half. Repeat with remaining wrap. Serves 2.

Note: If you don't like mayonnaise, you can substitute mustard or any of your favorite salad dressings (blue cheese and ranch work well).

Variation: Lightly coat the bottom of a heavy skillet with oil over medium-low heat. With only the turkey and cheese on the wraps, set them one at a time into the skillet. Cook until slightly brown and cheese is melted (about 3 minutes). Remove from pan and add remaining layers as directed above. Roll up and cut each wrap in half to serve.

If you are using a microwave, place wrap with cheese on a plate and heat for 30 seconds until cheese melts; add remaining layers. Roll up and cut in half.

Vegetarian variation: Omit the meat and try it with a smoked gouda or mozzarella cheese.

Ultimate Grilled Cheese Sandwich

This is true comfort food.

4 slices thick sour dough or country white bread

butter

4 thin slices ham

8 large basil leaves

4 slices smoked cheese

4 slices provolone cheese

4 thin slices tomato

salt and pepper to taste

2 tablespoons olive oil

Lightly butter 1 side of each bread slice. Place 2 bread slices, buttered side down, on work surface. Top each with 2 ham slices, then 4 basil leaves, then 2 slices of each cheese. Add two slices of tomato to each sandwich. Sprinkle with salt and pepper. Top with remaining 2 bread slices, buttered side up.

Heat olive oil in heavy large skillet over medium heat. Add sandwiches to skillet and cook until golden on bottom, about 4 minutes. Turn sandwiches over and cook until golden and cheese melts (about 5 minutes). Slice in half and serve. Serves 2.

Vegetarian variation: Omit the ham and use some drained roasted red peppers from a jar.

Cavender's Pasta Salad

The key to this tasty pasta salad is the Cavender's Greek seasoning and letting the flavors blend by refrigerating for at least 2 hours.

1 pound spaghetti
1 cup chopped black olives
1 cup chopped red bell pepper
1 stalk celery, chopped
½ cup chopped green onion

Break spaghetti in half and cook according to package instructions. Drain and rinse with cold water and place in a large bowl. Add black olives, red bell pepper, celery, and green onion and toss well. Pour Cavender's dressing over the spaghetti and toss to coat well. Refrigerate pasta for at least 2 hours before serving. Serves 6

Variation: Add 1 cup cooked chopped chicken breast.

Cavender's Greek Seasoning Dressing

1 cup mayonnaise
3 tablespoons olive oil
2 tablespoons lemon juice
3 tablespoons Cavender's seasoning (in the spice section of most grocery stores, usually on one of the lower shelves by the crab boils)

Whisk mayonnaise, olive oil, lemon juice, and Cavender's seasoning together in a small bowl; then pour over the spaghetti.

Low-fat variation: Substitute low-fat mayonnaise for regular.

Entrées

Southwest Beef or Turkey Burgers

These burgers are great for tailgating. Make them the night before and refrigerate for game day.

16 ounces ground beef or ground turkey

2 teaspoons Worchester sauce

1 clove garlic, minced

2 teaspoons cumin

1 teaspoon chili powder

1 teaspoon KC Masterpiece seasoning for beef or chicken

½ cup seasoned Italian bread crumbs

⅓ cup salsa

1 tablespoon olive oil for cooking on stovetop or grill

whole wheat buns

Combine meat with Worchester sauce, garlic, cumin, chili powder, KC Masterpiece seasoning, and bread crumbs. Mix well. Add the salsa and mix well. With your hands, form 3 to 4 patties.

Grill the patties on the grill, Foreman grill, or panfry them in olive oil over medium heat until desired doneness. Serves 3 or 4.

Cornflake-Crusted Chicken Fingers

Forget fast-food chicken fingers. These are moist on the inside and crispy on the outside.

3 boneless chicken breasts or a package of boneless breast tenders (about 12 ounces)

3 cups cornflakes

1 stick butter

1 teaspoon KC Masterpiece seasoning for chicken or regular seasoned salt

Preheat oven to 350°F.

If using boneless whole chicken breasts, cut chicken crosswise into pieces. If using boneless breast tenders, use as is.

Place the cornflakes in a large zip lock bag. Make sure there is no air in the bag. With the bag closed, crush the flakes using your fingers or place the bag on a cutting board and use a glass to crush them. Once crushed, place the corn-flakes on a plate.

Melt butter in a medium bowl and add the KC Masterpiece seasoning.

Dip each piece of chicken into the butter and then the cornflakes. Press the chicken into the cornflakes to make sure all sides are coated and place on a baking sheet. Repeat with remainder of chicken. Bake the chicken for 25 minutes. Serves 3–4.

Low-fat variation: Substitute light margarine for butter.

Easy Beef or Turkey Tacos

These no-fail tacos taste just like the ones you get at your favorite fast-food restaurant.

2 tablespoons olive oil

1 clove garlic, minced

1 pound ground beef or turkey

1½ teaspoons each chili powder and cumin
    (You can substitute by using one envelope of taco seasoning.)

4 tablespoons of your favorite salsa (optional)

¾ cup beef or chicken broth

taco shells or flour tortillas

grated cheese

salsa

chopped lettuce

sour cream

Heat olive oil over medium heat and add garlic. Cook 1 minute, taking care not to burn, and add the ground beef or turkey. Break the meat up with a wooden spoon and cook until all the meat is browned (about 6 minutes). Drain excess grease from meat and return pan to heat. Add the chili powder and cumin or taco seasoning packet and salsa. Stir well. Add the beef or chicken broth and cook over medium heat until the liquid has thickened.

Heat taco shells in the oven per the package instructions; for soft tacos, heat flour tortillas in the microwave for 30 seconds. Place 2 table-spoons of taco meat in each shell or tortilla, top with grated cheese, salsa, lettuce, and sour cream. Serves 4.

Note: Cook ground beef or turkey in microwave, stirring every minute for approximately 4–5 minutes until brown. Drain.

Comfy Shepherd's Pie

This English-style pub food is perfect for meat and potato lovers.

3 large russet potatoes

2 tablespoons olive oil

½ onion, chopped

1 large carrot, peeled and chopped

1 clove garlic, minced

1 pound ground beef or turkey

2 cups beef broth

½ cup frozen peas (optional)

½ cup milk

4 tablespoons butter

salt and pepper to taste

1 cup grated sharp cheddar cheese

Preheat oven to 350°F.

Fill a large saucepan three-quarters full of water, so as to allow room for the potatoes, and set on the burner. Peel potatoes and cut into chunks. Place into water and set the burner to high. Boil the potatoes for about 15 minutes until a fork inserted into potato goes in easily and potatoes are done.

While potatoes are cooking, heat oil over medium heat in a large skillet. Add the onion, carrot, and garlic, and sauté until fragrant but not brown (about 4 minutes). Add the ground beef or turkey, breaking it up with a wooden spoon, and cook until all parts are browned (about 6 minutes).

Drain the meat to strain off excess grease. Return pan to heat and add the beef broth. Simmer for 5 minutes until liquid thickens slightly. Add the frozen peas and stir to combine. Place meat in a square 9- x 9-inch baking dish and set aside.

Drain potatoes and return to the same pan. Add the milk and butter and mash with a potato masher or hand mixer until nice and smooth. Add more milk if desired, and salt and pepper. Stir in ¾ cup of the grated cheese, reserving remainder. Top meat with mashed potatoes. Sprinkle remaining cheese over the potatoes and bake in preheated oven for 30 minutes. Casserole should be bubbling, and potatoes should be nicely browned. Serves 4.

Baked Ziti with Tomato and Garlic

This easy, tasty recipe will satisfy your carb cravings and help you sleep.

1 pound ziti pasta

¼ cup olive oil

2 cloves garlic, minced

1 16-ounce can crushed tomatoes

salt and pepper to taste

½ cup Parmesan cheese

½ cup mozzarella cheese

Preheat oven to 400°F.

Place large pot of water on top of stove to boil with ½ teaspoon of salt. Cook pasta for only 7 minutes. It will be very al dente. Brush a 9- × 11-inch baking dish with olive oil. Drain the pasta and place in the baking dish. Pour olive oil over the pasta and toss lightly. Add the garlic and toss again.

Add the crushed tomatoes, salt, and pepper and mix until the pasta is evenly coated. Place a piece of aluminum foil coated with olive oil over the pasta and put into the preheated oven. Bake for 10 minutes; then open oven and stir pasta. Bake for another 15 minutes. Sprinkle cheese over the top and bake for another 5 minutes until cheese melts. Serves 4.

Variation: Sauté 1 chopped red bell pepper, 1 chopped onion, and 1 Italian sausage. Mix with crushed tomatoes and continue cooking according to instructions.

Pasta with Pesto Cream Sauce

Using store-bought pesto doesn't take away from this flavorful recipe.

12 ounces dry egg noodles or fettuccini pasta (can substitute any kind of fresh pasta)

3 tablespoons butter

1 cup heavy cream (also called whipping cream; look for in the dairy section)

2 tablespoons pesto sauce
  (look for in the deli section next to the fresh pasta or in the dairy section)

Parmesan cheese

Cook pasta according to package instructions. Drain. In the same pan, over medium heat add the butter and cook until melted and bubbly. Add the heavy cream and pesto. Stir to mix and return pasta to pan and stir to coat the pasta evenly. Sprinkle with Parmesan cheese. Serves 4.

Variation: Add 1 cup of cooked chicken, ½ cup diced sun-dried tomatoes, or a cup of your favorite steamed vegetables and stir to coat.

Low-fat variation: Omit the butter and use light cream or half-and-half or omit the cream completely.

Grilled Southwest Chicken with Black Bean Salsa

This is a very good recipe to make on a Foreman grill if you have one. You can also use the salsa in this recipe as a dip with tortilla chips.

3 lemons, juiced

¾ cup olive oil

1 teaspoon ground cumin

1 garlic clove, minced

4 boneless chicken breasts

1 can black beans, drained and rinsed

1 can whole-kernel yellow corn, drained

1 small red bell pepper, chopped

½ onion, chopped

¾ cup chopped fresh cilantro

1 lime, juiced

2 tablespoons olive oil

½ teaspoon sugar

salt and pepper to taste

Whisk together the lemon juice, ½ cup olive oil, cumin, and garlic in a small bowl. Place chicken breasts in a shallow dish and pour lemon juice mixture over the chicken. Let it marinate for at least 30 minutes—the longer the better.

While the chicken is marinating, drain and rinse the black beans and place in a medium bowl. Add the drained corn, red bell pepper, onion, and cilantro, and mix. Whisk together the lime juice, 2 tablespoons olive oil, sugar, salt, and pepper, and pour over the black bean mixture. Stir gently to coat with dressing.

Heat a regular grill or Foreman grill and cook the chicken about 10 to 15 minutes per side for a regular grill and about 5 to 7 minutes per side if using the Foreman grill. Place chicken on plates and spoon a generous serving of the black bean salsa over each one. Serves 4.

Variation: If you have leftover salsa, serve as a dip with tortilla chips for an appetizer or at a tailgating party.

Best Macaroni and Cheese

When the cupboard is bare or you want an easy dish for a Sunday supper, try this. It tastes like the mac and cheese Mom used to make, only easier. For balance, serve it with a nice salad.

8 ounces elbow macaroni

3 tablespoons butter

½ clove garlic, minced (optional)

½ cup milk plus 2 tablespoons

1½ cups Kraft Classic Melts grated cheese

½ teaspoon Tabasco sauce (optional)

2 slices thick bread, cut into cubes

½ clove garlic, minced

Preheat oven to 350°F.

Cook the macaroni according to package instructions and drain. Pour into a 9- × 9-inch buttered baking dish.

Meanwhile, in a small saucepan, melt 1 tablespoon butter. Add the minced garlic and stir for about 1 minute. Add the milk. When mixture begins to steam, not boil, add the cheese and stir until melted. Then add the Tabasco and stir to mix.

Pour cheese mixture over the macaroni and stir to coat all of the macaroni. Set aside.

Put bread cubes in a zip lock bag. Melt remaining 2 tablespoons butter, add garlic, and pour over the bread. Shake the bag gently until all the bread is coated with butter. Place the croutons on top of the macaroni and bake for 20 minutes or until bubbly and croutons are browned. Serves 3–4.

Variations: Add ½ cup cooked bacon/turkey bacon, smoked sausage or soy sausage and mix well. For vegetarians, add ½ cup cooked broccoli.

Low-fat variation: Substitute skim milk for whole milk; low-fat cheddar blend for Kraft Classic Melts; light margarine for butter.

Sides

Garlicky Mashed Potatoes

This version of mashed potatoes will have you coming back for seconds.

3 large russet potatoes

2 tablespoons butter

1 clove garlic, minced

¼ cup milk

½ cup sour cream

salt and pepper to taste

fresh chopped chives for garnish

Fill a large saucepan three-quarters full of water, so as to allow room for the potatoes, and set on burner. Peel potatoes and cut into chunks. Place into water and set the burner to high. Boil the potatoes for about 15 minutes until a fork inserted into potato goes in easily and potatoes are done.

Drain the potatoes. Put butter into the same saucepan and place over the warm burner. Add the garlic. Cook the garlic for 1–2 minutes; then add milk. Return potatoes to the pan. Add the sour cream. With a potato masher or hand mixer, mash potato mixture to a smooth consistency. Add salt and pepper. If you like your potatoes creamier, add more milk. Serves 2.

Variation: Add ½ cup cheddar cheese or blue cheese and mash as directed.

Grilled Corn on the Cob

This is an easy, no-nonsense way to cook corn on the cob, and it's delicious.

4 tablespoons butter, softened

1 clove garlic, minced

½ teaspoon chili powder

4 ears corn

salt and pepper to taste

Mix together the olive oil and garlic and set aside. Carefully pull back husks on corn without pulling them off. Remove the silk from the corn. Fold husks back into place. Place the corn in a large bowl and cover with cold water for 15 minutes.

Drain corn. Open one side of husks and pour 1 tablespoon of garlic olive oil over each piece of corn, season with salt and pepper, and fold husks back into place. Tie ends of corn with kitchen string or one of the outer husk layers. Set corn 5 to 6 inches over heat and grill for 15 minutes, turning occasionally. Wrap in foil to take to a tailgating party.

Variation: Remove husks and silk, wash and pat dry. Brush generously with garlic/chili butter, wrap in foil and bake in 350° oven for 35 minutes.

Home-Fried Potatoes

These potatoes will remind you of home.

2 large russet potatoes

1 medium onion

3 tablespoons olive oil

salt and pepper to taste

paprika for garnish

Peel potatoes and slice thinly. Peel onion and slice thinly. Heat oil in a large skillet over medium-high heat and add the potatoes and onion. Add salt and pepper. Fry potatoes and onion, turning frequently so as not to burn, until potatoes are tender. Sprinkle with paprika. Serves 2.

Garlic-Baked Broccoli

A new twist to liven up broccoli.

2 cups broccoli florets

1 cup seasoned Italian bread crumbs

1 clove garlic, minced

¼ cup olive oil plus 1 tablespoon

Preheat oven to 350F°. Place water in a saucepan with a steamer basket and turn heat to medium high. Add the broccoli, cover, and bring water to a boil. Cook for about 3 minutes, then drain and rinse under cold water to retain color. Pat dry and toss with 1 tablespoon olive oil. Then, mix bread crumbs, garlic, and olive oil together. Toss the broccoli in bread crumb mixture and place on a baking sheet. Bake for 10 minutes and serve. Serves 2.

Spinach Sautéed with Garlic, Pine Nuts, and Raisins

This is the Spanish version of sautéed spinach. The raisins and pine nuts add a sweet crunch to this dish.

½ cup water

1 12-ounce bag spinach or 4 cups packed spinach, rinsed and drained

2 tablespoons olive oil

1 clove garlic, minced

¼ cup pine nuts

¼ cup raisins

salt and pepper to taste

Place water in large skillet and add the spinach. Cook over high heat for about 2 minutes until spinach is wilted. Drain in colander. Heat oil in skillet and add the minced garlic. Cook until garlic begins to simmer but not brown. Add the spinach and sauté for about 2 minutes. Then add the pine nuts and raisins and mix. Season with salt and pepper. Serve immediately. Serves 3.

Desserts

Chocolate No-Bake Cookies

This recipe is great if you're craving something sweet and chocolaty but don't have an oven.

2 cups sugar

4 tablespoons unsweetened cocoa powder

½ cup whole milk

¼ cup (½ stick) unsalted butter

½ cup peanut butter (optional)

3 cups rolled oats (quick cooking)

1 teaspoon vanilla extract

Line a cookie sheet with waxed paper and set aside.

In a large, heavy-bottomed saucepan, combine the sugar and cocoa and mix well. Add the milk and butter and stir to combine. Cook over high heat, stirring constantly until mixture comes to a boil. Allow to boil for 2 minutes. Then remove from heat and stir in the peanut butter, add the oats and vanilla, and stir well to combine. Drop by tablespoonfuls onto the prepared cookie sheet and chill. Makes 4 to 5 dozen.

Chocolate-Dipped Strawberries

These are sure to impress your friends at parties and on tailgating Saturdays.

1 pint strawberries

1 cup milk chocolate chips

1 cup white chocolate chips

2 teaspoons vegetable oil

Line a cookie sheet with waxed paper and set aside.

Wash the strawberries and pat dry. Place milk chocolate chips and white chocolate chips in separate bowls. Add 1 teaspoon vegetable oil to each bowl. Place each bowl of chocolate in the microwave for 30-second intervals until the chocolate is melted to a nice smooth consistency. If chocolate is too thick, add a little more vegetable oil to thin.

Dip one strawberry at a time into milk chocolate and place on the cookie sheet. Repeat using the white chocolate. Let strawberries sit for about 10 minutes or refrigerate and then serve later.

Variation: Dip one side of strawberry in milk chocolate. Allow to set for a few minutes and then dip other side in white chocolate.

Strawberry Shortcakes

Great for a spring treat, and the best part is they only take a few minutes to put together.

1 package store-bought sponge cakes

1 pint strawberries

1 tablespoon sugar

1 tablespoon orange juice

1 cup heavy cream

1 teaspoon vanilla

Divide the sponge cakes among four plates. Clean the strawberries, remove stems and leaves, slice, and place in a bowl. Sprinkle sugar and orange juice over the strawberries and toss. Let the strawberries sit for about 10 minutes and stir again.

Meanwhile, whip the cream and vanilla using an electric mixer till soft peaks form. To serve, put a mound of strawberries on top of each sponge cake and top with a dollop of whipped cream. Serves 4.

Easy variation: If you don't have a hand mixer, just use Cool-Whip.

No More Munchapoloozas: Your Sophomore Year

By now you're probably sick of dorm food and you're certainly sick of trying to decipher exactly what kind of meat you're eating or wondering how old the vegetables are in the commissary. Now that you have one year under your belt, and assuming you can still fasten it, you're ready for the next level of cooking. If you skipped the Freshman recipes and instead found yourself with the junk food *munchapoloozas* or consuming *prozac shots,* no need to panic. Follow these recipes and you can get back on the right track.

You don't want the memories of those FLWs you heard yourself saying last year, "Just one more . . . anything . . . burrito, slice of pizza, scoop of ice cream . . ." haunting you. Funny how "just one more" can add up quickly. In this chapter you can substitute those high-fat favorites for some healthy, good-eat alternatives and you won't need to milk the *cash cow* to prepare them.

Lesson Plan: Prepare in advance. If you've just moved from the dorm and into an apartment, now is the time to accessorize your kitchen. Having the right utensils will save you time and make your life in the kitchen much simpler.

Cash cow: an ATM.

Munchapoloozas: consuming gross amounts of food.

Prozac shots: consuming cookie dough to lift your spirits.

Breakfast

Homeboy Egg and Cheese Muffins

Why go out when these only take a few?

4 slices bacon

2 English muffins, toasted

2 eggs, scrambled or over easy

1 tablespoon butter

2 slices cheddar cheese

Cook the bacon in a skillet or in microwave. If cooking in microwave, place bacon on a plate and cover with two paper towels for grease absorption and to avoid splatter (3–4 minutes). Set bacon aside.

Meanwhile, toast the muffins and place on two plates. Top each muffin with one slice of cheese. Heat butter in large nonstick skillet and break eggs into pan either for over easy or to scramble them. Put eggs on top of cheese and place 2 slices of bacon over eggs and top with other half of English muffin. Serves 2.

Low-fat variation: Substitute turkey bacon for bacon; Weight Watchers® English muffins for regular English muffins; light margarine for butter; low-fat cheddar for regular cheddar.

Buttermilk Pancakes with Cinnamon-Maple Apples

This is a healthy alternative to traditional pancakes with syrup.

1 cup all-purpose flour

1½ tablespoons sugar

½ tablespoon baking powder

¼ teaspoon salt

1 cup buttermilk

1 large egg, separated

1½ teaspoons vanilla extract

Whisk flour, 1 tablespoon sugar, baking powder, and salt in a large bowl to blend. Add buttermilk, egg yolk, and vanilla. Whisk until smooth (batter will be very thick). Using electric mixer, beat egg white in medium bowl to soft peaks. Add remaining ½ tablespoon sugar and beat until stiff but not dry; fold into batter.

Melt butter on griddle or in heavy large skillet over medium-low heat. Working in batches, pour batter by ¼ cupfuls onto griddle. Cook until pancakes are golden brown (about 3 minutes per side). Transfer to plates. Serve with cinnamon-maple apples. Makes about 12 pancakes.

Easy variation: If you don't have time to make these from scratch, use your favorite pancake mix and serve with cinnamon-maple apples.

Low-fat variation: Substitute low-fat buttermilk for regular buttermilk; light margarine for butter.

Cinnamon-Maple Apples

1 tablespoon (⅛ stick) unsalted butter

1 large Golden Delicious apple, peeled, cored, cut into ½-inch-thick slices

1 tablespoon maple syrup

½ teaspoon ground cinnamon

Melt butter in large nonstick skillet over medium-high heat. Add apples, maple syrup, and cinnamon; sauté until apples are tender (about 5 minutes). Add additional maple syrup as desired and serve on top of the buttermilk pancakes.

Cheesy Bacon Grits

These taste like the slow-cooked grits Grandma used to make.

1½ cups water

1½ cups milk

½ teaspoon salt

1 tablespoon unsalted butter

1 cup quick-cooking grits

½ cup shredded cheddar cheese

⅛ cup heavy cream

2 slices bacon, crumbled (turkey bacon also works well)

Heat water, milk, salt, and butter in a 3-quart heavy saucepan until it just begins to boil. Whisk in grits, lower the heat, and cook at a bare simmer, stirring constantly until grits are tender and thick. Add cheddar cheese. Stir in cream and bacon and remove from heat. Serve immediately. Serves 2.

Soups, Salads, and Starters

Old-Fashioned Chicken Noodle Soup

This is an easy recipe to double, so you'll have leftovers.

½ stick butter

1 onion, chopped

3 carrots, sliced

2 celery stalks, sliced

1 leek, chopped (use only the white part)

1 potato, diced

2 cups rotisserie chicken, cut into chunks

½ teaspoon thyme

4 cups chicken stock

salt and pepper to taste

Melt butter in a medium saucepan. Add onion, carrots, celery, leek, and potato. Sauté for about 10 minutes on medium heat. Add the chicken and thyme and stir. Reduce the heat to low, add the chicken broth, and stir. Cover and simmer for about 30 minutes until vegetables are soft. Add salt and pepper as desired. Serves 3.

Variation: To make your own chicken stock, remove most of the chicken from the bones and set aside for the soup. Place 4 cups of water in a large saucepan, add the chicken carcass, 1 onion cut into four sections, 2 stalks celery, 2 leeks, 2 carrots, and some salt and pepper. Bring to a boil, then reduce the heat and simmer for about 1 hour. Strain the liquid into a bowl and follow above recipe.

Hearts of Romaine with Blue Cheese, Pecans, and Lemon Vinaigrette

If you like elegant salads, try this one.

1 bag of romaine lettuce

½ cup grape tomato halves

3 ounces blue cheese, crumbled

¾ cup candied pecans, chopped (in the nut section of your grocery store)

Wash lettuce, strain, and place in a large salad bowl. Add the grape tomatoes and toss. Pour half of the lemon vinaigrette over lettuce and toss the salad. Divide the lettuce and grape tomatoes among 4 plates. Sprinkle with crumbled blue cheese and candied pecans. Drizzle a little more vinaigrette over top. Serves 4.

Cheaper variation: To candy your own pecans, heat 1 tablespoon butter in a skillet over medium heat. When butter melts, add 1 teaspoon sugar and stir. Then add pecans and toss well, coating all the pecans. Cook for about 3 to 5 minutes. Transfer to a plate covered with a paper towel and set aside to cool. They also make a great snack.

Lemon Vinaigrette

2 tablespoons fresh lemon juice

½ teaspoon sugar

salt and pepper to taste

5 tablespoons olive oil

Squeeze lemon juice into a measuring cup; remove any seeds (or squeeze lemon through your hand to strain the seeds). Add the sugar, salt, and pepper, and mix with a small whisk or fork. Add the olive oil and whisk until smooth.

Caprese Salad

This is the traditional Italian version of tomato, mozzarella, and basil salad.

2 tomatoes, sliced

2 rounds of fresh mozzarella cheese (usually found packed in water in the deli cheese case)

½ cup chopped fresh basil leaves

Slice tomatoes and place on a plate.

Slice mozzarella cheese and place one piece of cheese atop each tomato slice.

Sprinkle chopped basil leaves over the tomatoes and cheese, and drizzle the salad dressing on top. Serves 2–3.

Salad Dressing

1 tablespoon red wine vinegar

2 tablespoons olive oil

¼ teaspoon sugar

salt and pepper to taste

In a small bowl or measuring cup, whisk all ingredients together until blended.

Oriental Coleslaw

This is a delicious, crunchy twist on traditional coleslaw.

6 cups shredded cabbage or coleslaw (in the produce section along with the bagged lettuce)

½ cup roasted sunflower seeds

½ cup slivered almonds

½ cup raisins

3 green onions, chopped

1 package ramen noodles

3 tablespoons red wine vinegar

1½ tablespoons sugar

seasoning packet from ramen noodles

7 tablespoons olive oil

Place cabbage, sunflower seeds, almonds, raisins, and green onion in a large bowl and toss. Take the seasoning packet out of the ramen noodle package and set aside. Using your hands, break up the dry ramen noodles over the cabbage mixture and toss together. In a small bowl, whisk the vinegar, sugar, and seasoning for ramen noodles. Add the olive oil and whisk until well blended. Pour over the cabbage and toss well. Refrigerate for about 1 hour before serving. Toss before serving. Serves 6.

Cheesy Artichoke Dip

This is a great dip for parties, but don't expect leftovers.

1 can whole artichoke hearts, drained

1 jar marinated artichoke hearts, drained

1 2-ounce can mild green chilies, drained

1 cup Parmesan cheese

¾ cup mayonnaise

Preheat oven to 350°F.

Drain artichoke hearts. Chop and place in a medium baking dish. Add the green chilies, Parmesan, and mayonnaise. Mix well. Bake for 30 minutes or microwave for approximately 15 minutes, or until cheese is melted and dip is bubbling.

The Lighter Side

Quesadillas with Caramelized Onions

Caramelized onions give these quesadillas a rich flavor.

4 flour tortillas

1 onion, sliced thin

1 tablespoon olive oil

1 teaspoon sugar

2 teaspoons red wine vinegar

2 tablespoons salsa

½ cup grated cheddar cheese

½ cup cooked chicken, shredded

olive oil

In a small skillet sauté the onion with olive oil over medium heat until soft (about 10 minutes). Mix the sugar and vinegar together and add to the onions. Sauté for another 3 to 4 minutes until liquid thickens. Set aside. Place two tortillas on a cutting board. Spread 1 tablespoon salsa over each. Divide the cheese, chicken, and onions over each tortilla. Top with another tortilla. In a large skillet heat a small amount of olive oil over medium heat. Place one of the quesadillas in the skillet and toast on one side. Carefully flip it over and toast the other side. Cut into triangles and serve. Serves 2.

Vegetarian and low-fat variation: Use low-fat cream cheese instead of cheddar. Mix with 2 tablespoons chopped black olives, 2 tablespoons chopped pimientos, and 1 tablespoon dried or fresh chives. Spread over tortilla, add caramelized onions, and cook as directed.

Grilled Turkey Reuben

Smoked turkey is a cheap substitute for the traditional corned beef used in Reubens.

2 slices good rye bread (can substitute whole wheat or white bread or pumpernickel)

butter for spreading

1 tablespoon Russian dressing (look for in the salad dressing aisle)

3 thin slices smoked turkey breast

2 slices Swiss cheese

¼ cup sauerkraut, well-drained

Spread one slice of bread with butter. Turn over and spread with ½ tablespoon of the Russian dressing. Top with cheese, turkey, sauerkraut, and another slice of cheese. Butter other slice of bread and turn over. Spread that slice with remainder of the Russian dressing and place on top of cheese, turkey, sauerkraut, and cheese. Heat a skillet over medium and place sandwich in pan. Grill on one side and then turn over and grill the other side. Serves 1.

Crunchy Chicken Salad

Apples and pecans add a sweet crunch to this recipe.

2 boneless chicken breasts

4 cups water

2 chicken bouillon cubes

¾ cup chopped celery

¼ cup minced onion

¾ cup chopped pecans

½ cup chopped apple

Place water and bouillon cubes in a large saucepan and bring to a boil. Add the chicken, reduce the heat, and simmer for 20–25 minutes until chicken is cooked through. Drain the chicken and cool. Chop chicken into chunks and place in a medium bowl. Add the celery, onion, pecans, and apple. Pour dressing over the chicken and mix well. Serve chicken over lettuce or on bread or rolls. Serves 2–3.

Variation: You can substitute rotisserie chicken, using only the breast meat, to make this recipe quicker.

Dressing

1 cup sour cream

3 tablespoons chopped parsley

1½ tablespoons red wine vinegar

½ teaspoon sugar

½ teaspoon celery seed

½ teaspoon salt

pepper to taste

Place sour cream in a small bowl with the parsley. In a separate bowl, whisk together the vinegar, sugar, celery seed, salt, and pepper. Then mix with the sour cream and parsley with a whisk. Pour over above recipe.

Low-fat variation: Substitute low-fat or fat-free sour cream for regular sour cream.

Black Bean Veggie Burgers

These burgers are a healthy, low-fat alternative to traditional burgers.

1 15- to 16-ounce can black beans, rinsed and drained

⅓ cup chopped red onion

⅓ red bell pepper, chopped

⅓ cup canned whole-kernel corn, drained

1 cup Italian bread crumbs

2 tablespoons plus ½ cup bottled chunky salsa

1 teaspoon ground cumin

½ teaspoon hot pepper sauce (such as Tabasco)

salt and pepper to taste

2 whole wheat buns

In a medium bowl, mash three-fourths of the beans. Add the onion, red bell pepper, corn, ½ cup bread crumbs, 2 tablespoons salsa, cumin, and hot pepper sauce. Season with salt and pepper. Mix together well and then add the rest of the black beans. Gently mix.

Rub hands with a little olive oil and make 2 4-inch-diameter patties. Place remaining bread crumbs on a plate. Dip black bean patties in seasoned bread crumbs. Rub Foreman grill with oil and grill for about 3 minutes per side; or put a little oil in a skillet over medium heat and cook for 3 minutes per side. Transfer burgers to bottom half of bun, top each burger with ¼ cup salsa, and place top of bun to serve. Serves 2.

Entrées

Vegetarian Chili

For all you vegetarians out there, here is a chili you can make for tailgating.

3 tablespoons olive oil

1½ cups diced onion

2 cloves garlic, minced

1 red bell pepper, diced

2 carrots, peeled, trimmed, and diced

1 cup frozen corn

1 teaspoon salt

3 teaspoons chili powder

3 teaspoons cumin

½ teaspoon oregano

1 28-ounce can crushed tomatoes with liquid

2 cups tomato puree

¾ cup vegetable stock

2 14-ounce cans black beans, rinsed and drained

½ cup shredded cheddar cheese (optional)

½ cup sour cream (optional)

½ cup chopped cilantro (optional)

Heat oil in a heavy large saucepan over medium heat. Add onion, garlic, red bell pepper, carrots, and corn. Cook, stirring until the onion is lightly browned (about 8–10 minutes). Sprinkle salt over vegetables, and add the chili powder, cumin, and oregano. Cook until fragrant. Pour in the tomatoes and liquid, tomato puree, and stock and stir. Bring to a boil.

Adjust the heat so that the liquid is simmering. Cover and cook until the vegetables are very tender (about 10 minutes). Add the black beans and cook until heated through. Serve hot in bowls, passing the cheddar cheese, sour cream, and cilantro for topping. Serves 3–4.

Key Lime Shrimp on the Grill

The marinade gives these shrimp their succulent texture.

24 large shrimp, peeled and deveined

¾ cup key lime juice (can be found in the baking section at most grocers)

3 cloves garlic, minced

1 teaspoon lime or lemon pepper

1 teaspoon sugar

½ cup olive oil

Peel and devein the shrimp. Place in a strainer and rinse under cold water. Set aside to drain. In a large bowl whisk together lime juice, garlic, seasoned pepper, sugar, and olive oil. Add the shrimp and marinate for 1 hour. Using four metal or wooden skewers (if using wooden skewers, soak in cold water while shrimp marinates), put six shrimp on each skewer. Heat the grill on medium and place the shrimp on the grill. Grill for about 3–6 minutes on one side and then turn over and grill another 2–3 minutes, depending on thickness of the shrimp. Serves 3–4.

Savory Sweet and Sour Meatballs

This is a great do-ahead recipe.

Sauce

1 tablespoon olive oil

1 cup finely chopped onion

2 large cloves garlic, minced

1 28-ounce can crushed Italian-style tomatoes

1 cup beef broth

½ cup (packed) golden brown sugar

juice of 1 lemon

Heat olive oil in a heavy large saucepan over medium heat. Add onions and garlic and cook until onions are soft (about 8 minutes). Pour in tomatoes with their juice, broth, brown sugar, and lemon juice. Stir well and bring to a boil. Reduce heat to low and simmer sauce while preparing meatballs.

Meatballs

1 pound lean ground beef or turkey

1 onion, finely chopped

2 cloves garlic, minced

½ cup Italian bread crumbs

1 teaspoon salt

½ teaspoon ground pepper

½ teaspoon allspice

1 large egg, beaten slightly

¼ teaspoon red pepper flakes

Preheat oven to 400°F.

Place a large sheet of parchment paper over a baking sheet. Set aside. In a large bowl, combine beef or turkey, onion, garlic, bread crumbs, salt, pepper, and allspice. Add egg; blend well. Shape mixture into 1- to 1½-inch balls. Bake the meatballs on lined baking sheet for about 40 minutes, turning once during cooking. (Make sure to use parchment paper and not aluminum foil, which sticks.) Once done, gently drop meatballs into simmering sauce. Partially cover pot and simmer over very low heat for about 45 minutes. Spoon off any fat from top of sauce. Serve over noodles or rice or as an appetizer. (Can be made 2 days ahead. Cover; chill. Rewarm over low heat before serving.) Makes about 22.

Dad's Beer-Marinated Grilled Steak

The longer you marinate these steaks, the juicer they'll be.

1 can any light or dark beer

½ cup light soy sauce

2 tablespoons Worchester sauce

1 clove garlic, minced

½ cup olive oil

salt and pepper to taste

2 good-quality steaks

Whisk together first six ingredients. Place steaks in a shallow dish and pour marinade over them. Marinate for at least 3 hours, turning twice during the 3-hour period. Heat grill to high. Once hot, sprinkle steaks with salt and pepper and sear on one side for about 6 minutes. Turn over and cook until desired doneness. Serves 2.

Variation: Mix together a tablespoon of butter and 2 ounces of blue cheese until creamy. Put a dollop on each hot steak before serving.

Pizza with Goat Cheese, Red Bell Peppers, and Artichoke Hearts

The combination of flavors gives this pizza a gourmet twist.

1 Boboli thin-crust pizza shell (can be found in any grocery store) or frozen pizza dough

½ cup tomato sauce (Prego Organic Tomato Basil is good)

3 tablespoons olive oil

1 clove garlic, minced

½ red bell pepper, sliced into strips

1 cup frozen artichoke heart quarters

3 ounces chèvre (goat) cheese, crumbled

Preheat oven to 400°F.

Place pizza crust on a pizza pan. Spread the tomato sauce over the crust. Set aside. Heat the olive oil in a skillet over medium heat. Add the garlic and simmer until fragrant. Add the red bell pepper and artichoke hearts and sauté until both vegetables are softened (about 10 minutes).

Place the vegetables on top of the pizza and sprinkle with the goat cheese. Bake for about 10 minutes. Serves 3–4.

Variation: The fun thing about making pizza is that you can put just about anything you want on it. Try fresh tomatoes and crispy bacon, or spinach and feta cheese.

Pasta Shells with White Clam Sauce

This is a simple way to make a traditional Italian white clam sauce.

3 tablespoons butter

½ cup olive oil

1 large onion, chopped

1 clove garlic, minced

1 teaspoon dried oregano

1 teaspoon dried parsley

½ cup white cooking wine

juice of half a lemon

2 6-ounce cans minced clams with juice

16 ounces medium-sized pasta shells

¼ cup Parmesan cheese

salt and pepper

Place a large pot of water with a little salt on the stove and bring to a boil. Meanwhile, heat butter and oil in a large skillet over medium heat. Add onion and garlic and cook until onions are soft (about 8 minutes). Add oregano and parsley and stir. Turn heat to medium high and add the white wine and lemon juice. Cook until liquid is reduced slightly. Add the clams with their juice and cook until thickened slightly (about 4 minutes). Reduce heat to simmer.

Add pasta shells to boiling water and cook according to package instructions. When pasta is done, drain and pour back into same pot. Add Parmesan to clam sauce and stir well. Pour clam sauce over shells and toss well. Serve with additional Parmesan sprinkled on top. Serves 4.

Pasta Alfredo with Chicken, Asparagus, and Tomatoes

If you're looking for comfort food, this pasta will hit the spot.

1 16-ounce package ziti pasta

1 bunch asparagus

3 tablespoons olive oil

2 cloves garlic, minced

1 cup grape tomato halves

2 cups rotisserie chicken, cut into cubes

3 tablespoons butter

1¼ cups heavy cream

1 cup Parmesan cheese

Bring a large pot of water to a boil for the pasta. Cook pasta according to package instructions. Cut off the woody ends of the asparagus (about 1 inch from bottom); then cut asparagus into three pieces. Heat olive oil in a large skillet over medium heat. Add the garlic and cook until fragrant (about 30 seconds). Add the asparagus and cook for about 8 minutes, stirring often. Add tomatoes and chicken to skillet and cook for another 3 minutes. Drain the pasta and place the pan back on the stove over medium-low heat. Add butter and 1 cup heavy cream to the pan and stir until butter is melted. Add pasta back to pan and stir to coat. Add the vegetable and chicken mixture to the pasta and toss. Add the Parmesan and the rest of the heavy cream. Serve immediately. Serves 4.

Low-fat variation: Substitute light margarine for butter and light cream for heavy cream.

Curried Couscous with Veggies

This favorite of my daughter's is great for vegans.

2 cups vegetable stock

1 cup couscous

4 tablespoons olive oil

1 clove garlic, minced

½ onion, chopped

½ red bell pepper, chopped

1 cup frozen corn

½ cup black olive halves

1 cup chickpeas, drained (optional)

½ cup green peas

1 teaspoon curry powder

½ teaspoon ground turmeric (optional)

Bring vegetable stock to a boil. Stir in the couscous, remove from heat, and cover. Let stand while you cook vegetables. Heat olive oil in large skillet over medium heat. Add the garlic, onion, and red bell pepper. Sauté for about 8 minutes. Add the corn, black olives, chickpeas, green peas, curry powder, and turmeric and stir until vegetables are coated. Add the couscous to the skillet and stir to break up and mix in vegetables. Drizzle with more olive oil if mixture seems dry. Serve immediately or at room temperature. Serves 3.

Sides

Oven-Roasted Potatoes with Garlic, Rosemary, and Parmesan Cheese

Serve these potatoes with any grilled meat or fish.

2 large potatoes

3 tablespoons olive oil

2 cloves garlic, minced

1 tablespoon whole rosemary

½ cup Parmesan cheese

Preheat oven to 400°F.

Cut potatoes into thick slices and then cut again into quarters. Rinse under cold water and pat dry with paper towels. Place potatoes in a large zip lock bag. Add the olive oil, garlic, and rosemary, and shake the bag to coat the potatoes.

Spray a cookie sheet or baking dish with non-stick oil or rub with olive oil. Place potatoes on the cookie sheet or baking dish and bake for about 20 minutes. Stir the potatoes. Bake for another 20–25 minutes until potatoes are golden brown. Sprinkle Parmesan over potatoes and bake for another 3 minutes until cheese is melted. Serves 2–3.

Dilled Potato Salad

This is not your traditional potato salad; the sour cream adds a smooth richness.

3 large potatoes, unpeeled

½ cup minced onion

½ cup fresh dill, minced (use 1 teaspoon dry dill as a substitute)

1 cup sour cream

2 tablespoons red wine vinegar

1 teaspoon salt

½ teaspoon pepper

Bring a large pot of water to a boil over high heat. Add the potatoes whole. Boil the potatoes until you can pierce easily with a fork (about 20–25 minutes). Place potatoes in a strainer and rinse under cold water. Let stand to cool.

Peel potatoes and cut into slices or chunks, whichever you prefer. Place in a large bowl. Meanwhile, in a small bowl, mix together the onion, dill, sour cream, vinegar, salt, and pepper. Whisk together until smooth. Pour over potatoes and gently turn until all the potatoes are coated. Garnish with more fresh dill. Refrigerate for 1–2 hours before serving. Serves 4–6.

Low-fat variation: Substitute fat-free sour cream for regular sour cream.

Creamed Corn Casserole

This dish is a Thanksgiving favorite, but you can make it year-round.

2 eggs, beaten

2 tablespoons flour

1 tablespoon sugar

2 tablespoons butter

1 cup milk

2 cans whole-kernel corn, drained

½ cup diced onion

salt and pepper to taste

10 to 12 crushed Ritz crackers mixed with 1 tablespoon melted butter

Preheat oven to 350°F.

Whisk together eggs, flour, sugar, butter, and milk. Add corn, onion, and salt and pepper. Pour into a buttered baking dish and top with buttered crackers. Bake for 45 minutes. Serves 4.

Grandma's Green Beans

This is a nice alternative to boiling or steaming green beans.

3 slices bacon (can substitute turkey or soy bacon)

1 onion, cut into large chunks

1 pound flat green beans

1 teaspoon salt

½ teaspoon pepper

½ cup chicken broth

Trim the green beans by removing each end and tearing off string. Snap the beans in half or thirds, depending on how long they are. Rinse under cold water.

In a large heavy skillet over medium high heat, cook the bacon until fat is rendered and bacon is slightly crisp. (If using turkey or soy bacon, you will need to add 2 tablespoons olive oil.) Remove bacon and add the onion, beans, salt, and pepper to the skillet, toss to coat, then cover and reduce heat to low. Cook beans for 3–3½ hours, stirring occasionally. If beans begin to stick, add ½ cup of chicken broth, cover, and continue cooking. Serves 4–5.

Desserts

Old-Fashioned Granola Bars

You'll never want store-bought granola bars again after you've tried these.

4 cups old-fashioned oats (slow-cooking)

1 cup packed seedless raisins

1 cup chopped pecans

½ cup unsalted sunflower seeds (optional)

2 teaspoons cinnamon

1½ sticks butter

⅔ cup packed dark brown sugar

5 tablespoons honey

1 teaspoon vanilla

Preheat oven to 350°F. Line a 9- × 13-inch baking pan with foil, allowing foil to extend over the sides. Butter the foil.

Mix together the oats, raisins, pecans, sunflower seeds, and cinnamon in a large bowl. Place butter, brown sugar, and honey in a small saucepan. Heat over medium heat until butter melts and mixture begins to bubble. Add vanilla and mix well. Pour butter mixture over oat mixture and stir until well coated. Transfer to prepared pan. Using a spatula, press mixture evenly into pan. Bake about 30 minutes until top is golden brown. Transfer to a rack and cool. Using foil as an aid, lift out of the pan and place on a work surface. Cut into 18 bars and place in an airtight container for storing.

Decadent Chocolate Brownies

Once you make these, a mix will never do.

⅔ cup butter

1½ cups sugar

¼ cup water

1 12-ounce package chocolate chips

2 teaspoons vanilla

4 eggs

1½ cups flour

½ teaspoon baking soda

1 cup chopped pecans (optional or substitute pecans for walnuts)

Preheat oven to 325°F. Butter and flour a 9- × 13-inch baking pan.

In a saucepan, combine butter, sugar, and water. Bring to a boil over medium heat. Remove from heat and add the chocolate chips and vanilla, stirring until the chips are melted and mixture is smooth.

Transfer melted chocolate to a large bowl and add the eggs one at time, mixing well after each addition. Add the flour and baking soda to the chocolate and stir gently with a whisk to combine. Do not overbeat. Add the nuts and stir to combine. Pour mixture into prepared pan and bake for about 50 minutes or until a toothpick inserted in the middle comes out clean. Pour icing over hot brownies and garnish with chopped pecans.

Icing

2 tablespoons butter

2 tablespoons milk

½ cup sugar

1 cup semisweet chocolate chips

½ cup chopped pecans

Melt butter with the milk. Add sugar. When mixture begins to bubble, remove from heat and add the chocolate chips. Stir until melted. Pour immediately over hot brownies. Sprinkle with chopped pecans.

Apple Cake with Vanilla Sauce

This warm treat is great for a cold fall or winter day.

4 cups Granny Smith apples, peeled, cored, and cut into small chunks

1¾ cups sugar

2 cups flour

2 teaspoons cinnamon

½ teaspoon salt

1½ teaspoons baking soda

¾ cup vegetable oil

2 eggs, beaten

1 teaspoon vanilla

1 cup chopped pecans

Preheat oven to 350°F. Butter and flour a 9- × 13-inch metal baking pan.

Place apple chunks in a large mixing bowl. Add the sugar and toss to coat the apples. Add remaining dry ingredients; stir well to coat all the apples.

In a separate bowl, beat oil, eggs, and vanilla. Stir egg mixture into apple mixture. Add pecans and stir until moistened into a thick batter. Pour the batter into prepared pan and bake for 50 minutes or until fork inserted in the middle comes out clean. Prepare vanilla sauce.

Vanilla Sauce

6 tablespoons butter

¾ cup sugar

½ cup heavy cream

1 teaspoon vanilla

In a small saucepan, melt the butter over medium heat. Add the sugar and heavy cream and stir constantly until the sugar is dissolved and sauce is a smooth consistency (about 5 minutes). Remove from heat and stir in the vanilla. Serve sauce warm over each slice of apple cake.

Chocolate Peanut Butter Balls

This recipe will satisfy your craving for peanut butter cups.

1 stick unsalted butter

2 cups creamy peanut butter (do not use old-fashioned style or freshly ground)

1 cup dry milk powder

1½ cups powdered sugar

1 12-ounce package milk chocolate chips

1 tablespoon vegetable oil

Line a cookie sheet with wax paper. Melt butter in a small saucepan over low heat. Combine peanut butter, dry milk, and powdered sugar in large bowl. Mix in butter. Moisten hands and roll 1 tablespoon of mixture into a ball. Place on prepared cookie sheet. Repeat with remaining mixture. Chill overnight or place in freezer for at least an hour.

Line another cookie sheet with wax paper. Melt chocolate chips in double boiler over low heat, stirring occasionally. Add vegetable oil and stir well. Remove chocolate from over water. Using a fork, dip peanut butter balls one at a time into chocolate and transfer to prepared cookie sheets. Refrigerate until chocolate is firm. (Can be prepared one week ahead. Refrigerate in airtight container.) Makes 24–30.

Dreamy Lemon Bars

These light, airy bars are perfect for a summer picnic.

1½ sticks (¾ cup) unsalted butter

2 cups all-purpose flour

½ cup plus 3 tablespoons powdered sugar

4 large eggs

1½ cups granulated sugar

2 teaspoons lemon zest

¾ cup fresh lemon juice

⅓ cup all-purpose flour

Preheat oven to 350°F.

Cut butter into ½-inch pieces and place in a large bowl. Add the flour and ½ cup powdered sugar. With a pastry cutter or fork, mix together until it begins to form small lumps. Sprinkle the mixture into a 9- × 13-inch baking pan and press the mixture to bottom of pan. Bake in the middle of the oven until golden brown (about 10 minutes). Meanwhile, whisk together the eggs, sugar, lemon zest, lemon juice, and flour. Pour lemon mixture over hot shortbread crust and bake until set (25–30 minutes). Cool completely in the pan. Cut into bars and then sift remaining 3 tablespoons powdered sugar over top of lemon bars. Makes 24.

Banana Nut Bread with Chocolate Chips, Blueberry Muffins & Smoothies *(pages 94, 62 & 2)*

Buttermilk Pancakes with Cinnamon-Maple Apples *(page 31)*

Turkey Wraps *(page 10)*

Caprese Salad *(page 35)*

Quesadillas with Caramelized Onions & As You Like It—Mexican Salsa *(pages 38 & 5)*

Stuffed Italian Mushrooms *(page 99)*

Grilled Turkey Reuben & Creamy Corn Salad *(pages 39 & 118)*

Spicy Black Bean Soup & Pan con Tomate *(pages 67 & 7)*

Warm Goat Cheese Salad with Honey and Pecans *(page 68)*

Cheesy Crabmeat Toasts *(page 71)*

Stadium Chili *(page 72)*

Cornflake-Crusted Chicken Fingers & Garlicky Mashed Potatoes *(pages 14 & 21)*

Grilled Southwest Chicken with Black Bean Salsa *(page 19)*

Best Macaroni and Cheese *(page 20)*

Pizza with Goat Cheese, Red Bell Peppers, and Artichoke Hearts *(page 47)*

Pasta Alfredo with Chicken, Asparagus, and Tomatoes *(page 49)*

Rigatoni with Tomato and Black Olive Sauce *(page 74)*

Dad's Beer-Marinated Grilled Steak & Twice-Baked Cheesy Potatoes *(pages 46 & 83)*

Authentic Cheese Enchiladas *(page 81)*

Spanish Shrimp Scampi *(page 105)*

Three-Cheese Lasagna *(page 112)*

Chicken Stuffed with Goat Cheese in Mushroom Marsala Sauce *(page 108)*

Asparagus Bundles Wrapped in Prosciutto *(page 85)*

Tortilla Española (Spanish potato frittata) *(page 114)*

Strawberry Shortcakes *(page 28)*

Chocolate No-Bake Cookies *(page 26)*

Decadent Chocolate Brownies *(page 56)*

Chocolate-Orange Squares & Chocolate-Dipped Strawberries *(pages 91 & 27)*

Key Lime Pie *(page 88)*

White Chocolate Cheesecake *(page 122)*

Vanilla Is No Longer the In Flavor: Your Junior Year

Whew! You made it, dude. Two years down, two to go. The next two years could mean more *demics,* which could translate to more *all-nighters.* But pots of coffee and Red Bull aren't the answer. If you find yourself becoming a *mouse potato,* take a break. Get into the kitchen with friends and cook up a nice healthy meal to see you through until morning.

These recipes are not *vanilla.* You'll find they are not only delicious but pretty easy to make, too. And when it comes to FLWs this year, the old, "I told you this course was easy" applies to these recipes, but not to your course in economics or medieval Europe. You're not in grade school anymore, so read on if you have a craving for some good food.

Lesson Plan: Stay away from the vending machines. Candy bars and salty snacks are not the answer. Make an effort this year to cook in at least four nights a week. Take time to figure out a menu plan for the week and make one trip to the grocery store. This will open up more time for you to study and prepare healthy meals for yourself.

All-nighters: all-night study sessions.

Demics: short for "academics"; what you came to school for.

Mouse potato: someone who's addicted to the computer.

Vanilla: very plain or having no excitement.

Blueberry Muffins

Great for on-the-go breakfast eaters.

¾ stick (6 tablespoons) unsalted butter, melted and cooled

¾ cup packed light brown sugar

½ cup milk

1 large egg

1½ cups all-purpose flour

1½ teaspoons baking powder

1½ teaspoons cinnamon

½ teaspoon salt

2 cups blueberries (7½ ounces)

Optional Topping

Combine the following ingredients with a fork or pastry cutter:

2 tablespoons flour

¼ teaspoon cinnamon

2 tablespoons oatmeal

1 tablespoon butter

Put oven rack in middle position and preheat oven to 400°F. Place 12 (½ cup) muffin cup liners in a muffin pan.

Whisk together butter, brown sugar, milk, and egg in a bowl until combined well. Whisk together flour, baking powder, cinnamon, and salt in a large bowl. Add milk mixture and stir until just combined. Fold in blueberries gently.

Divide batter among cups, sprinkle topping over batter, and bake until golden brown (25–30 minutes) or until a toothpick inserted in center of a muffin comes out clean. Makes 12.

Variation: If fresh blueberries aren't available, use frozen. You can even use blackberries if you prefer. Defrost them first and follow recipe.

Macadamia Nut and Banana Pancakes with Caramel Butter

Spend a weekend indulging yourself with these pancakes.

Caramel Butter

1 stick butter	¼ cup water
¾ cup sugar	¾ cup heavy cream

Place butter in skillet and melt over low heat. Add the sugar and water; turn the heat to high. Stir the mixture constantly until it boils and mixture thickens and turns a dark tan (about 3–4 minutes). Once mixture is dark tan, immediately remove from the heat and whisk in the heavy cream. Set aside to cool while you make the pancakes.

Pancakes

1½ cups all-purpose flour	4 tablespoons unsalted butter, melted
2 tablespoons sugar	2 large eggs
1½ teaspoons baking powder	1½ teaspoons vanilla
½ teaspoon baking soda	1 ripe large banana
¼ teaspoon salt	½ cup chopped salted roasted macadamia nuts
1¾ cups well-shaken buttermilk	(2½ ounces)

Whisk together flour, sugar, baking powder, baking soda, and salt in a bowl. Whisk together buttermilk, 3 tablespoons melted butter, eggs, and vanilla in a large bowl until smooth. Add flour mixture and whisk until just combined. Cut banana into bits and fold into batter along with nuts.

Brush a 12-inch nonstick skillet with some of the remaining tablespoon melted butter and heat over moderate heat until hot but not smoking. Working in batches of 3, pour ¼ cup batter per pancake into hot skillet and cook until bubbles appear on surface and undersides are golden brown (1–2 minutes). Flip pancakes with a spatula and cook until golden brown and cooked through (1–2 minutes more). Transfer to a large plate and loosely cover with foil to keep warm; then make more pancakes, brushing skillet with butter for each batch. Serve with caramel butter. Makes 15 (4-inch) pancakes.

Easy and cheap variations: Substitute walnuts or pecans for macadamia nuts. And if you don't have time to make the pancakes from scratch, you can use your favorite pancake mix and fold banana and nuts into mixture. Then serve with the caramel butter.

Tip: If you have any leftover caramel, put it over vanilla ice cream or frozen yogurt for a tasty dessert.

Bacon, Cheese, and Tomato Omelet

Omelets are easy; the key is a good nonstick skillet.

4 large eggs

2 tablespoons milk

¼ teaspoon salt

¼ teaspoon ground black pepper

2 tablespoons (¼ stick) butter

2 slices bacon cooked until crisp, crumbled

½ cup chopped tomatoes

½ cup grated Gruyère cheese, packed

Beat eggs, milk, salt, and pepper in small bowl to blend. Melt 1 tablespoon butter in small nonstick skillet over medium-high heat. Add half of egg mixture to skillet. Cook until eggs are just set in center, tilting pan and lifting edge of omelet with spatula to let uncooked portion flow underneath (about 2 minutes). Top half of omelet with half of the crumbled bacon, half of the tomatoes, and half of the cheese. Using spatula, fold other half of omelet over cheese and cook about 30 seconds more. Slide the omelet onto a plate. Repeat with remaining butter, egg mixture, bacon, tomatoes, and cheese. Makes 2 omelets.

Low-fat and vegetarian variation: Substitute turkey or soy bacon for bacon; light margarine for butter; low-fat Swiss for Gruyère cheese.

Soups, Salads, and Starters

Spicy Black Bean Soup

This soup will take the chill off a cold winter day.

2 tablespoons olive oil

1 small onion, chopped

1 red bell pepper, chopped

1 stalk celery, chopped

2 cloves garlic, chopped

1 jalapeño pepper, seeded and chopped

3 cans black beans

1½ tablespoons ground cumin

2 teaspoons ground coriander

Salt and pepper to taste

1 tablespoon hot sauce

4 cups (or more) vegetable stock or canned vegetable broth

1 15-ounce can diced tomatoes

½ lime, juiced

1 cup coarsely chopped fresh cilantro

Sour cream

Heat oil in a medium soup pot over medium-high heat. Add onion, red bell pepper, celery, garlic, and jalapeño. Cook 10 minutes, stirring occasionally. Drain and rinse 2 cans of beans and add them to pot. Drain and rinse third can of beans. Place in a bowl and mash with a fork. Stir the mashed beans into the pan and add the cumin, coriander, salt and pepper, and hot sauce. Add stock and tomatoes to the soup and bring to a bubble. Reduce heat and simmer 15 minutes over low heat. Add the lime juice. Stir in the cilantro. Serve with a dollop of sour cream sprinkled with additional cilantro. Serves 6.

Tip: Serve this hearty soup with the Sweet Southern Cornbread in this chapter.

Warm Goat Cheese Salad with Honey and Pecans

The honey adds a perfect sweetness to the tangy goat cheese.

4 slices whole wheat bread, toasted (cut a round from center of each slice using a round cookie cutter)

1 3- to 4-ounce log of soft mild goat cheese such as Montrachet, cut into 4 slices

1 bag Boston or mixed lettuce, washed well

1 cup grape tomato halves

Vinaigrette

2 tablespoons fresh lemon juice, or to taste

1 tablespoon chopped chives

1 teaspoon Dijon-style mustard, or to taste

½ teaspoon sugar

salt and pepper to taste

⅓ cup walnut oil (available at specialty foods shops) or olive oil

¾ cup pecan halves

Honey

In a small bowl whisk together the lemon juice, chives, mustard, sugar, salt, and pepper. Add the oil in a stream, whisking until mixture is blended.

Preheat broiler. Toss the salad with tomatoes, pecans, and dressing and divide among 4 plates.

Place one slice of goat cheese on top of each bread round and place on a cookie sheet. Broil until the cheese begins to brown slightly around the edges. Watch carefully so that cheese doesn't burn (about 3 minutes). Place one round on top of each salad and drizzle honey over cheese. Serve immediately. Serves 4.

Citrus-Marinated Shrimp

These shrimp, tangy and sweet, are great for a large party.

1 pound cooked peeled large shrimp

1 box shrimp boil (located in the spice section at the grocery store)

½ cup orange juice

½ cup fresh lemon juice

½ cup ketchup

¼ cup vodka (optional; see variation)

¼ teaspoon hot pepper sauce

2 tablespoons olive oil

½ small red onion, thinly sliced (about 1¾ cups)

¾ cup finely chopped fresh cilantro

Place a large pot of water on stove with the shrimp boil. Turn on high and bring water to a boil. Add the shrimp and cook for only 4 minutes. Drain the shrimp. When they are sufficiently cool, peel and devein them. Set aside.

In a large bowl whisk together the orange juice, lemon juice, ketchup, vodka, and hot pepper sauce. Add the olive oil and whisk until mixture is combined and thick. Add the shrimp, onion, and cilantro; mix well. Cover and refrigerate for at least 2 hours and up to 7 hours. Serves 4.

Variation: Substitute white cooking wine, located with the vinegars in the grocery store, for the vodka if you're not yet of age to buy liquor.

The Lighter Side

Easy Quiche Lorraine

Premade piecrust makes this dish a cinch.

1 9-inch store-bought piecrust

2 teaspoons flour

6 large eggs

⅔ cup heavy cream

1 cup milk (preferably whole)

salt and pepper to taste

8 ounces Gruyère, Emmentaler, or other Swiss-type cheese

¼ teaspoon freshly ground nutmeg (optional)

2 slices bacon cooked until crisp, crumbled

½ cup chopped chives (optional)

Preheat oven to 425°F.

Unroll piecrust and sprinkle with flour. Using your fingers, spread the flour around the crust. Place the crust in a pie dish, floured side down. Fold edges under, and using your fingers, crimp the edges all the way around. Poke the bottom with a fork and place the pastry in the freezer for 30 minutes.

In a medium-size bowl, whisk together the eggs, cream, and milk until thoroughly blended.

Season with salt and pepper, then add the cheese and stir until it is blended. Pour the mixture into the prepared crust and sprinkle with nutmeg, bacon, and chives. Place in the oven and back for about 30 to 40 minutes. To test for doneness, shake the quiche: if it is solid, without a pool of uncooked filling in the center, it is done. You may also stick a sharp knife blade into the center of the filling, and if it comes out clean, the quiche is baked through. Serves 6.

Cheesy Crabmeat Toasts

Make this for a quick midweek meal.

2 tablespoons unsalted butter

¼ cup finely chopped red bell pepper (optional)

1 green onion, finely chopped

2 3-ounce cans white crab meat, drained

2 tablespoons fresh lemon juice

1 egg beaten

1 teaspoon Worcestershire sauce, or to taste

¼ cup mayonnaise

1 teaspoon Dijon-style mustard

½ teaspoon hot pepper sauce

½ cup grated Parmesan cheese

4 English muffins, halved and toasted

In a skillet, heat the butter and cook the bell pepper and onion over moderately low heat, stirring, until the vegetables are softened. Remove from the heat and stir in the crabmeat, lemon juice, egg, Worcestershire sauce, mayonnaise, mustard, hot pepper sauce, and Parmesan cheese and divide the crab-meat mixture among the muffin halves, spreading to the edges and mounding it slightly. Sprinkle the sandwiches with additional Parmesan and broil them under a preheated broiler about 4 inches from the heat for 3–4 minutes, or until the tops are golden. Serves 4.

Low-fat variation: Substitute light margarine for butter; light mayonnaise for regular mayonnaise; low-fat cheddar for Parmesan; Weight Watchers English muffins for regular muffins.

Stadium Chili

Unsweetened cocoa powder adds a rich, velvety taste to this chili recipe.

4 tablespoons olive oil

1 large onion, chopped

3 cloves garlic, minced

1½ pounds ground beef or ground turkey

3 tablespoons chili powder

2 tablespoons ground cumin

1 tablespoon unsweetened cocoa powder

1 teaspoon cinnamon

1 teaspoon oregano

3 cups beef broth

2 16-ounce cans pureed tomatoes

1 tablespoon sugar

salt and pepper to taste

1 16-ounce can kidney beans, rinsed and drained

Cheddar cheese

purple onion, chopped

A handful chopped fresh cilantro

Heat olive oil in a large saucepan over medium heat. Add onion and garlic and cook for about 10–15 minutes until onions are soft. Add the beef or turkey and cook until all the meat is browned (about 8 minutes). Using a strainer, drain the grease from the meat and return to pan. Add the chili powder, cumin, cocoa powder, cinnamon, and oregano and stir well. Add the beef broth, pureed tomatoes, sugar, and salt and pepper. Add the kidney beans and stir well. Reduce heat to low and continue cooking for 20 minutes, stirring occasionally. Garnish with cheddar cheese, purple onion, and a sprinkle of cilantro. Serves 6.

Philly Cheese Steak Sandwiches

When you eat these, it's easy to imagine being in Philadelphia.

1½ pounds top round steak

4 tablespoons extra-virgin olive oil

2 medium Vidalia or other sweet onion, sliced thin, then in half

5 bell peppers, any color, sliced thin, then in half

1 clove garlic, minced

Salt and pepper to taste

¼ pound sharp provolone cheese, thinly sliced

4 to 6 soft hero rolls or hoagie rolls

Tightly roll the round steak into a torpedo or log shape. Wrap tightly in plastic. Place log in freezer for 45 minutes to firm the beef into a tight, but not frozen, texture.

Remove plastic and, working quickly, slice the beef into the thinnest slices possible, and then flatten the slices using a meat mallet. Refrigerate slices until ready to cook.

While meat is in the fridge, make pepper and onion mixture. In a large skillet, heat olive oil over medium-high heat. Sauté onion, peppers, and garlic; add salt and pepper and cook until onion and peppers are tender (about 15–20 minutes). Transfer mixture to a bowl and set aside.

In the same skillet, panfry steak in two batches until brown but not crispy. To serve, place hoagie rolls on a cookie sheet covered with foil. Add meat, then warm onions and peppers, and top with provolone cheese. Place under the broiler for 30 seconds until cheese is melted. For tailgating, wrap sandwiches in foil and take in an insulated carrier to keep warm. Serves 4–6.

Rigatoni with Tomato and Black Olive Sauce

This is a no-fuss, delicious topping for pasta.

5 large tomatoes, chopped

1 can small black olives, drained

1½ teaspoons salt

¼ cup olive oil

12 ounces rigatoni pasta

Parmesan cheese

Place tomatoes and olives in a casserole dish that will fit in your microwave. Sprinkle tomatoes and olives with salt and drizzle the olive oil on top. Poke the mixture with a spoon to incorporate the olive oil slightly, but don't stir it. Place the dish in the microwave and cook on high for 15 minutes. Stir the mixture slightly, adding a little more olive oil if needed, and cook another 10–15 minutes.

Meanwhile, cook the pasta according to package instructions and drain. Place the pasta in a large bowl. Add the tomato sauce and toss to mix well. Divide into bowls and sprinkle with Parmesan cheese. Serves 3.

Cheaper, easier variation: Substitute 1 16-ounce can chopped tomatoes for fresh tomatoes.

Stove-Top Barbecued Pork Chops

These are great for a rainy day when the grill is off limits.

4 pork loin chops, cut about 1 inch thick

4 tablespoons flour

salt and pepper to taste

2 tablespoons olive oil

1 cup beef bouillon

Dredge pork chops with flour mixed with salt and pepper. Heat oil in skillet on medium heat. Brown pork chops on both sides. Pour bouillon over pork, cover, and reduce heat to simmer. Cook pork chops for 30 minutes. Drain off most of the liquid, leaving about 4 tablespoons. Add the barbecue sauce and continue to simmer for another 30 minutes until pork is tender.

Classic Barbecue Sauce

3 tablespoons olive oil

1 large onion, finely chopped

2 cloves garlic, minced

1 lemon

½ cup dark brown sugar

¼ cup vinegar

¾ cup tomato ketchup

1 tablespoon Worcestershire sauce

½ teaspoon Tabasco sauce, or to taste

¼ teaspoon chili powder, or to taste

Heat the oil in a frying pan and sauté the onion and garlic until soft and lightly browned (4–5 minutes). Grate the zest from the lemon and squeeze the juice. Add the lemon zest, half the lemon juice, the brown sugar, vinegar, ketchup, Worcestershire sauce, Tabasco sauce, and chili powder to the onion and simmer gently (5 minutes). Pour mixture over the pork chops as instructed above.

Variation: You can grill pork chops and use barbecue sauce for basting.

Mom's Pot Roast with Caramelized Onion Gravy

The caramelized onion gravy is a sweet variation on this traditional pot roast.

¼ cup flour

1 teaspoon salt

¼ teaspoon pepper

4 pound rump of beef

4 tablespoons olive oil

2 cloves garlic, minced

½ cup red cooking wine

1 cup beef bouillon

1 cup pureed tomatoes

1 tablespoon finely chopped rosemary
  (or 1 teaspoon dried)

3 carrots, scraped and sliced thick

2 large potatoes, cut into thick chunks

2 tablespoons olive oil

3 large onions, sliced thin

2 teaspoons sugar

¼ cup red wine vinegar

½ cup beef bouillon

salt and pepper to taste

Position rack in middle of oven and preheat to 350°F.

On a large plate, mix flour with the salt and pepper and roll the meat until all of it is covered with flour. Heat 3 tablespoons of the olive oil over medium heat and add the meat. Brown on all sides and then place the meat in a roasting pan. In the same pan, heat remaining olive oil and add the garlic. When sizzling, but not brown, add the red wine, beef bouillon, pureed tomatoes, and rosemary. Bring to slight simmer and then pour over the meat. Cover tightly with foil and bake for 2½ hours until very tender. After meat has been cooking for 1 hour, add the carrots and potatoes to the roasting pan, cover, and continue cooking for remaining 1½ hours.

Make Caramelized Onions

During final 30 minutes of roasting, in heavy 12-inch skillet over moderately high heat, heat 2 tablespoons olive oil until hot, but not smoking. Add onions and sugar and sauté, stirring occasionally (about 20 to 25 minutes). Add vinegar, beef bouillon, salt and pepper, and cook until liquid is gone. Keep warm.

Make Gravy

When beef is tender, transfer to serving platter and tent with foil. Skim fat from liquid in pot. Strain liquid through fine-mesh sieve, pressing on solids with back of spoon to extract all juices; discard solids. You should get about 2 cups of liquid. If not, add some beef bouillon to the mixture to make 2 cups.

In a large skillet, heat 2 tablespoons olive oil over medium heat. With a wire whisk, add 2 tablespoons of flour and mix until thickened to a paste (about 1 minute). Slowly whisk in the 2 cups of reserved liquid, making sure to whisk the lumps as you're pouring in the broth. Bring to a boil. Reduce heat, season juices to taste with salt and freshly ground black pepper, and add the caramelized onions to the gravy. Slice the meat and serve with caramelized onion gravy.

Shrimp and Spinach in Tarragon Cream Sauce

If you have the money to splurge and want to impress that special someone, try this recipe.

14 uncooked large shrimp, peeled and deveined

2 tablespoons chopped fresh Italian parsley

olive oil

2 tablespoons fresh lemon juice

4 teaspoons chopped fresh tarragon, divided

1 teaspoon peeled and minced fresh ginger

salt and pepper to taste

½ cup finely chopped shallots (about 2 large)

3 tablespoons butter

½ cup heavy cream

1 clove garlic, minced

1 package fresh baby spinach, steamed and set aside

Toss shrimp, parsley, 1 tablespoon olive oil, 1 tablespoon lemon juice, 2 teaspoons tarragon, and minced ginger in medium bowl. Sprinkle mixture with salt and pepper.

In a medium skillet, heat 1 tablespoon olive oil over medium heat. Add shallots and sauté (6 minutes). Add shrimp mixture and sauté until shrimp are almost cooked through (about 3 minutes). Add butter, cream, and remaining lemon juice; bring just to simmer. Season with salt and pepper. Keep warm.

Meanwhile, heat 1 tablespoon olive oil in another large nonstick skillet over high heat. Add garlic and cook until garlic simmers. Add spinach and sprinkle with salt and pepper. Toss until heated through (about 30 seconds). Mound spinach in center of plates; ladle shrimp with the sauce over the spinach and serve. Serves 2.

Low-fat variation: Substitute light margarine for butter; light cream for heavy cream.

Spaghetti with Hearty Bolognese Sauce

Nothing beats a good plate of spaghetti.

2 tablespoons olive oil

1 medium onion, chopped

2 carrots, coarsely chopped

2 stalks celery, coarsely chopped

3 cloves garlic, finely chopped

½ pound each of ground beef and pork

1 cup red wine

½ cup beef bouillon

1 tablespoon balsamic vinegar

2 14½-ounce cans diced tomatoes

2 2-ounce cans tomato paste

2 tablespoons fresh basil chopped
  (can substitute 2 teaspoons dry basil)

2 tablespoons fresh oregano chopped
  (can substitute 2 teaspoons dry oregano)

1 tablespoon sugar

Salt and pepper to taste

1 pound spaghetti

Grated Parmesan cheese

Heat oil in heavy large saucepan over medium-high heat. Add onion, carrot, celery, and garlic; sauté until soft (about 8 minutes). Add the ground beef and pork and cook until all the meat is brown (about 8 minutes). Drain off the fat and replace pan on the heat. Add wine, bouillon, and balsamic vinegar and cook, stirring often (about 3 minutes). Stir in tomatoes with juice, tomato paste, basil, oregano, and sugar. Season with salt and pepper. Reduce heat to low, cover, and simmer until thickened (about 45 minutes).

Meanwhile, cook pasta in large pot of boiling salted water until tender but still firm to bite. Drain and divide among 4 plates. Spoon sauce over pasta and sprinkle with Parmesan cheese. Serves 4.

Chicken with Lemon Wine Sauce

This is a simple variation on chicken piccata.

2 skinless boneless chicken breasts, pounded thin

1 egg, beaten

½ cup seasoned Italian bread crumbs

2 tablespoons olive oil

1 clove garlic, minced

1 cup white wine

1½ teaspoons lemon zest

4 tablespoons lemon juice mixed with 1 teaspoon sugar

fresh parsley, chopped

Dip each chicken breast in egg and then seasoned bread crumbs. Set aside.

Heat olive oil in heavy skillet over medium heat. Add the garlic and simmer for 30 seconds; then add the chicken to the skillet. Brown chicken on both sides (about 2–3 minutes per side). Add the white wine, lemon zest, and lemon juice mixture, and cook uncovered for about 3 minutes. Reduce the heat to simmer and continue cooking until chicken is tender and cooked through (about 20 minutes). Garnish with fresh chopped parsley. Serves 2.

Authentic Cheese Enchiladas

It's hard to find good Mexican food, so why not make your own? You won't be disappointed with these.

14 corn tortillas

4 tablespoons olive oil

3 cloves garlic, minced

3 tablespoons flour

3 tablespoons chili powder

3 tablespoons cumin

3 cups chicken or vegetable bouillon

3½ cups shredded cheddar and Monterey Jack cheese

1 cup chopped cilantro

sour cream and cilantro to garnish

Preheat oven to 350°F. Grease a 9- × 11-inch baking dish with oil and set aside.

In a heavy nonstick skillet, toast the tortillas on both sides, one at time. Stack on a plate and set aside.

Heat the olive oil in a skillet over medium heat. Add the garlic and cook for about 1 minute, but don't brown. Whisk in the flour, chili powder, and cumin; mix well to form a paste. Very slowly, a little at a time, add the bouillon, whisking well after each addition until all the bouillon is added and no lumps appear. Continue cooking until the sauce thickens slightly (about 5 minutes). Turn off the heat.

In a large bowl, mix together the cheese and cilantro and set aside. Working on a cutting board, dip a tortilla in the sauce and let excess sauce drip back into pan. Lay tortilla on a cutting board, sprinkle cheese at bottom of tortilla, and roll up. Place seam side down in oiled baking dish. Repeat with remaining tortillas. Once all tortillas are in the pan, pour the remainder of the sauce over the enchiladas and sprinkle with remainder of the cheese mixture. Bake for 30 minutes until bubbly. Garnish with a dollop of sour cream sprinkled with cilantro. Serves 4–5.

Low-fat variation: This is a low-fat recipe to begin with, but if you want to reduce the calories even more, substitute low-fat cheddar and Monterey Jack for regular cheese.

Variation: Add some shredded chicken, tofu, or refried beans (red kidney or pinto are good) to each enchilada.

Tofu Stir-Fry

Who knew tofu could be this good? Marinating ahead of time is the key.

3 cups firm tofu, cut into 1¼-inch cubes
    (blocks of tofu packed in water are usually displayed in the produce section)

Marinade

2 tablespoons rice wine

1 cup soy sauce

½ teaspoon chili sauce

1 clove garlic, minced

2 cups canola oil for frying, plus 3 tablespoons

1 sweet onion, sliced

2 cloves garlic, minced

1 cup thinly sliced carrots

1 cup broccoli florets

1 pint grape tomatoes, cut in half

3 tablespoons rice wine

½ cup green onions cut into inch-long pieces

salt to taste

Marinate the tofu for 1–2 hours and drain, reserving liquid. Heat 2 cups canola oil in a deep frying pan. Working in batches, deep-fry the cubes of tofu until golden brown, making sure they don't stick to each other. Wait between batches for oil to return to 375°. Drain tofu on paper towels.

Heat a wok or large skillet over high heat until hot. Add 3 tablespoons canola oil. Add onion, garlic, and carrots, and cook for 2 to 3 minutes, stirring constantly. Add broccoli and cook for about 6 minutes, continuing to stir. Add tomatoes and cook, stirring carefully, just until tomatoes begin to soften (about 1–2 minutes). Deglaze with rice wine and cook for approximately 1–2 minutes. Add the tofu and green onions, stir, and season with salt to taste. Add approximately ½ cup reserved liquid and cook for another minute. Serve over steamed rice. Serves 4.

Sides

Twice-Baked Cheesy Potatoes

Serve these with your favorite grilled meat or eat them alone.

3 slices bacon cooked until crisp, chopped

3 medium russet potatoes, scrubbed,
each pierced several times with fork

¼ cup (½ stick) butter

¼ cup whole milk

½ cup sour cream

½ cup chopped chives

1 cup grated cheddar cheese, divided

1 teaspoon salt

¼ teaspoon pepper

Preheat oven to 400°F.

Bake all potatoes in microwave on high until tender, about 10 minutes per side, turning once after 5 minutes. Wrap the potatoes in foil and let them rest for 10 minutes. Cut potatoes lengthwise. Let cool slightly. Cut an edge around the inside of each potato half. Then scoop cooked potato flesh into a medium bowl, leaving ¼-inch-thick potato shell. Add butter, milk, sour cream, and chives to potato flesh in bowl and mash well. Stir in bacon, ½ cup cheddar cheese, salt, and pepper. Spoon potato mixture into shells. Place potatoes on baking sheet. Sprinkle remaining ½ cup cheddar cheese over tops of potato halves.

Bake potatoes in preheated oven until filling is heated through and shells are crisp (about 30–40 minutes).

Low-fat and vegetarian variation: Eliminate bacon or substitute turkey or soy bacon for regular bacon; light margarine for butter; light or fat-free sour cream for regular sour cream; low-fat cheddar for regular cheddar.

Artichokes Sautéed with Garlic and Parmesan

The secret is to use frozen artichokes. They're the next best thing to fresh.

1 bag frozen artichoke hearts

3 tablespoons olive oil

2 cloves garlic, chopped

1 cup Parmesan cheese

Place frozen artichokes in a glass bowl and microwave for 2 minutes to defrost slightly. Drain.

Heat olive oil in a large skillet over medium heat and add the garlic. When garlic is sizzling, add the artichokes and toss. Continue cooking, stirring frequently for about 15 minutes until artichokes are nicely braised. Sprinkle Parmesan cheese over artichokes and place a lid on the pan for about 3 minutes until cheese is melted slightly. Serves 4.

Asparagus Bundles Wrapped in Prosciutto

This makes an impressive side to any dish.

20 medium asparagus spears

1 tablespoon olive oil

1 clove garlic, minced

salt and pepper to taste

4 large thin slices prosciutto (⅓ pound)

Preheat oven to 350°F.

Mix together the olive oil and garlic and season with salt and pepper. Trim asparagus by cutting off the hard stems so that they are about 5 inches long, and then steam over boiling water until crisp-tender (about 3 minutes). Drain and immediately refresh under cold water to stop the cooking and retain color. Drain and pat dry. Lay one piece of the prosciutto on a piece of wax paper. Take 5 asparagus spears and bundle them at one end of the prosciutto slice. Carefully roll the prosciutto around the asparagus bundle and place seam side down in an oiled baking dish. Repeat with remaining asparagus and prosciutto. Brush each bundle with garlic and olive oil mixture and bake for 15 minutes. Serves 4.

Note: You can find prosciutto in the deli section at any major grocery store. Just ask the attendant to give you four thin slices. It should only cost you a couple of bucks.

Variation: After steaming and wrapping prosciutto, just drizzle with lemon vinaigrette (see page 34) and serve at room temperature.

Broccoli with Creamy Cheese Sauce

Nothing goes better with broccoli than a creamy cheese sauce.

2 cups broccoli florets

1 tablespoon butter

⅓ cup milk

1½ cups grated casserole cheese (such as Kraft Classic Melts)

1 tablespoon olive oil

1 clove garlic, minced

Steam broccoli for about 4 minutes. Drain into a colander and refresh with cold water. Meanwhile, in a small saucepan over medium heat, melt butter. Add milk and then grated cheese; stir until all the cheese is melted. In a skillet, heat olive oil over medium heat. Add the garlic and then the broccoli and cook for about 4 minutes more. Divide onto two plates and pour cheese over each serving. Serves 2.

Low-fat variation: Substitute low-fat cheese for regular cheese; light margarine for butter.

Sweet Southern Cornbread

For a filling meal, serve this with any soup or salad.

¾ cup all-purpose flour

¾ cup yellow cornmeal

⅓ cup honey

1½ teaspoons salt

1½ teaspoons baking powder

1 teaspoon baking soda

½ cup thinly sliced green onions

1¼ cups buttermilk

2 large eggs

6 tablespoons unsalted butter, melted and cooled

Preheat oven to 350°F. Butter 13- × 9-inch metal baking pan.

Whisk flour, cornmeal, honey, salt, baking powder, and baking soda in large bowl to blend. Stir in green onions.

Whisk buttermilk and eggs in medium bowl to blend, then whisk in melted butter. Add buttermilk mixture to dry ingredients and stir just until blended (do not overmix). Transfer batter to prepared pan. Bake cornbread for about 25 minutes or until a toothpick inserted in the middle comes out clean. Serves 10.

Variation: Add ½ cup drained canned or frozen corn and 1 tablespoon chopped jalapeño pepper.

Desserts

Key Lime Pie

This perfect light dessert is especially good after a spicy meal.

1¾ cups graham cracker crumbs (or use a prepared graham cracker crust)

2 tablespoons sugar

6 tablespoons unsalted butter, melted

1 (14-ounce) can sweetened condensed milk

5 large egg yolks

½ cup plus 3 tablespoons fresh or bottled key lime juice (if using bottled, preferably Manhattan brand)

¾ cup chilled heavy cream

1 teaspoon sugar

Lime zest

Preheat oven to 350°F.

Stir together graham cracker crumbs and sugar. Then add the butter and mix with a fork until combined well. Press mixture evenly onto bottom and up sides of a 9-inch (4-cup) glass pie pan. Bake crust for 5 minutes and remove from oven, but leave the oven on.

In a medium bowl, whisk together the condensed milk and egg yolks. Beat well for about 5 minutes. Add the key lime juice and whisk until well combined. Pour filling into pie crust and bake for 15 minutes. Cool pie completely and then refrigerate for at least 5 hours. Just before serving, beat together the heavy cream with 1 teaspoon sugar until fluffy. Serve pie with a dollop of whipped cream and grated lime zest. Or, if you're feeling creative, pipe whipped cream around the edge of the pie. Serves 6–8.

Variation: Spread whipped cream over top of pie and freeze for a tasty, refreshing dessert.

Easy Chocolate Mousse

Don't let the idea of mousse scare you away from this recipe. It's simple and delicious.

2 cups heavy cream

4 large eggs, separated

½ cup sugar

¼ cup (½ stick) unsalted butter, cut into ½-inch pieces

¼ cup water

pinch of salt

1 teaspoon vanilla

10 ounces semisweet chocolate, chopped

Heat ¾ cup of the heavy cream in a 1-quart heavy saucepan until hot, but not boiling.

In a metal bowl, whisk together yolks, sugar, butter, water, and salt until combined well. Then add hot cream in a slow stream, whisking until combined. Transfer mixture to saucepan and cook over moderately low heat, stirring constantly, until it registers 160°F on thermometer. Pour custard through a fine-mesh sieve into a bowl and stir in vanilla.

Heat 8 ounces (1 cup) of the chocolate in a glass bowl in the microwave in 30-second intervals until chocolate is melted, stirring frequently. Whisk the chocolate into the custard until smooth and then cool completely.

Beat the remaining 1¼ cups of cream with an electric mixer until it just holds stiff peaks. Whisk one-fourth of whipped cream into chocolate mixture to lighten. Then fold in remaining whipped cream gently but thoroughly. Spoon mousse into individual cups or stemmed glasses. Sprinkle with remaining 2 ounces of chopped chocolate. Serves 6–8.

Grandma's Blueberry–Apple Crisp

The word "Grandma" says it all here—a sweet taste from home.

1 cup firmly packed golden brown sugar

2 teaspoons ground cinnamon

8 cups Granny Smith apples, peeled, cored, cut into chunks

2 cups blueberries, stems removed, washed

3 tablespoons lemon juice

Topping

1 cup all-purpose flour

1 cup quick oats

⅔ cup sugar

1 teaspoon cinnamon

½ cup (1 stick) chilled unsalted butter, cut into pieces

Preheat oven to 400°F. Butter 13- × 9-inch glass baking dish.

Combine brown sugar and cinnamon in large bowl. Add apples, blueberries, and lemon juice and toss to coat. Transfer apple mixture to prepared dish.

For the topping, mix flour, oats, sugar, cinnamon, and butter in medium bowl. Using pastry blender or fingertips, blend ingredients until coarse meal forms. Spread flour mixture evenly over apples and blueberries. Bake for 20 minutes. Reduce the heat to 350°F and bake for another 30 minutes. Let stand 15 minutes before serving.

Variation: Substitute peaches for apples.

Chocolate-Orange Squares

Chocolate and orange go so well together in these quick and easy bars.

1 packaged roll of sugar cookie dough (found in refrigerated section of the grocery store)

1 16-ounce jar of good-quality orange marmalade

1 cup semisweet chocolate chips

1 tablespoon milk

Preheat oven to 350°F.

Let the cookie dough stand at room temperature for about 30 minutes. Then spread it out in the bottom of a 9- × 13-inch baking pan. Bake the crust about 10 to 15 minutes until it's a nice golden color. Remove from the oven and spread the orange marmalade over it. Heat the chocolate with the milk in the microwave or over low heat on the stove until melted. Drizzle the chocolate over the marmalade and refrigerate for at least an hour. Cut into squares. Makes 16 bars.

Variation: Use raspberry jam instead of orange marmalade.

Knocking Yourself Out: Your Senior Year

This is it dude, the year you graduate! You're studying like crazy and you'll probably hear the FLWs, "I just have to make an A on the final to pass," a lot. This is a favorite, watching your friends calculate, refigure, and compute what's needed to get the grade they want or desperately need to pass. Then there's "I'll just borrow their notes," while assuming that the friend is not a Neanderthal with a 1.7 GPA. If you're studying, eating properly, and not being a *bag monster*, you'll be able to pass without fail.

The recipes in this chapter may be a little more involved, but you're no newbie, and I'm sure you can *bone up* to the challenge. So knock yourself out and invite your friends over for a meal that they will be talking about until graduation. They'll be asking you if they can have a copy of your recipe, not your notes.

Lesson Plan: This is your last year unless you're planning on continuing to graduate school, so make it a healthy one. Cook, cook, cook. You're about to go out into the real world of work, where you'll most likely be setting up a permanent residence somewhere. Take what you've learned and really hone in on your cooking skills. Cooking can be fun and rewarding. Accomplishing that difficult recipe is somewhat like passing that history test. You'll feel like you've achieved something and you'll be proud of yourself.

Bag monster: student who sleeps all day.

Bone up: to prepare for a challenge.

Breakfast

Banana Nut Bread with Chocolate Chips

The chocolate chips will satisfy your sweet tooth.

2 cups all-purpose flour

1 teaspoon baking soda

1 teaspoon baking powder

¼ teaspoon salt

¾ cup semisweet chocolate chips

½ cup walnuts, toasted, chopped

1 stick unsalted butter, room temperature

1 cup sugar

2 large eggs

3 ripe bananas, mashed

2 tablespoons fresh lemon juice

2 teaspoons vanilla extract

Preheat oven to 350°F. Butter and flour a 9- × 5- × 2½-inch metal loaf pan.

Whisk first 4 ingredients in medium bowl to blend. Combine chocolate chips and walnuts in small bowl; add 1 tablespoon flour mixture and toss to coat.

In a large bowl, using a hand mixer, beat butter in large bowl until fluffy. Gradually add sugar and beat until well blended. Beat in eggs 1 at a time. Beat in mashed bananas, lemon juice, and vanilla extract. Mix in flour mixture. Spoon ⅓ of batter into prepared pan. Sprinkle with half of nut mixture. Spoon ⅓ of batter over. Sprinkle with remaining nut mixture. Cover with remaining batter. Run knife through batter in zigzag pattern.

Bake bread until knife inserted into center comes out clean (about 1 hour 5 minutes). Turn out onto rack and cool.

Low-fat/reduced calorie variation: Omit the chocolate chips and substitute one cup of Splenda for the sugar.

Eggs Benedict

Don't be intimidated by the hollandaise sauce. If you follow these instructions, you'll do just fine.

4 large eggs, separated

1 tablespoon cream

1 tablespoon lemon juice

dash of cayenne pepper

½ teaspoon salt

2 sticks butter, melted

2 English muffins

4 slices Canadian bacon, cooked

4 eggs

For hollandaise sauce, whisk yolks, cream, lemon juice, cayenne pepper, and salt in top of double boiler over simmering water (water should never boil) until slowly dissolving ribbon forms when whisk is lifted and thermometer registers 140°F, or mixture is as thick as heavy cream (about 4–5 minutes). Gradually whisk in melted butter, about 1 teaspoon at a time, until thick and smooth. Keep warm in top of double boiler over warm water while eggs are cooking.

Fill a large skillet with water about 2 inches deep. Bring water to boil, then reduce heat to simmer.

Toast the muffins and set on two plates. Place a piece of Canadian bacon on each muffin half. Crack eggs into skillet of simmering water. Cook until whites are set and yolks are set to desired doneness (about 3 minutes for medium-set yolks). Using slotted spoon, transfer eggs, placing one egg on each muffin half. Spoon a generous serving of hollandaise over each muffin and serve immediately. Serves 2.

Spinach and Mushroom Frittata

This is a great dish for a Saturday or Sunday brunch.

2 cloves garlic, minced

1½ tablespoons olive oil

1 cup sliced mushrooms

4 cups (packed) fresh spinach leaves, chopped, or 2 cups frozen chopped spinach, thawed, drained, and squeezed

6 large eggs

½ teaspoon salt

¼ teaspoon pepper

1 cup Swiss cheese, shredded

Preheat broiler.

Cook 1 clove garlic in oil in a 10-inch well-seasoned cast iron or other ovenproof skillet over moderate heat for about 1 minute. Add mushrooms and cook until all the liquid is absorbed and mushrooms begin to brown (about 10 minutes). Remove the mushrooms from the pan and set aside. Add a little more olive oil to the same pan and second clove of garlic. Sauté for 1 minute and add the spinach. Cover with a lid until spinach wilts (about 1–2 minutes). Remove lid and continue cooking until any liquid is absorbed. Return the mushrooms to the pan, season with salt and pepper, and stir to mix.

While spinach is cooking, whisk together eggs, salt, and pepper until combined, then pour over spinach and mushrooms in skillet. Cook, undisturbed, over moderate heat until almost set (5–6 minutes). Sprinkle cheese evenly on top and broil 4 to 5 inches from heat until eggs are just set and cheese is melted (1–2 minutes). Serves 4–6.

Soups, Salads, and Starters

French Onion Soup

This soup is sure to satisfy your craving for this traditional French treat.

½ stick butter

5 onions, sliced

5 cloves garlic, minced

¾ cup white wine

3 cups chicken broth

3 cups beef broth

1 teaspoon Dijon mustard

salt and pepper to taste

12 slices French bread, toasted

1¼ cups Swiss or Gruyère cheese

In a large pot over medium heat, melt the butter. Add the onions and garlic and sauté until very tender and brown (about 45 minutes). Add the wine and simmer until reduced to a glaze (about 3 minutes). Add the broths and mustard, and stir well. Season with salt and pepper. Simmer for 10 minutes.

Preheat broiler.

Ladle the soup into four broiler-proof bowls. Top each with three slices of French bread and grated cheese. Broil until cheese melts and bubbles. Serves 4.

Sun-Dried Tomato and Goat Cheese Crostini Salad

The goat cheese crostini gives this salad a gourmet look and taste.

1 bag mixed lettuce greens

⅔ cup chopped and drained sun-dried tomatoes packed in oil

½ cup chopped walnuts

4 ounces soft goat cheese

1 tablespoon chopped chives (can use dried chives if you want)

4 thinly baguette slices

Vinaigrette

2 tablespoons fresh lemon juice

1 teaspoon sugar

Salt and pepper

5 tablespoons olive oil

Preheat the broiler.

Place mixed lettuce greens in a large bowl. Add sun-dried tomatoes and walnuts; set aside. In a separate small bowl mix together the goat cheese and chives. Place baguette slices on a baking sheet and spread each slice with goat cheese mixture.

Vinaigrette

Measure lemon juice into a small bowl. Add the sugar, salt, and pepper and mix with a small whisk or fork. Add the olive oil and whisk until smooth. Toss the greens with sun-dried tomatoes and walnuts with vinaigrette and divide among four plates.

Place baguette slices with goat cheese and chives under broiler until cheese begins to brown around the edges (about 2–3 minutes). Place one crostini on top of each salad and serve immediately. Serves 4.

Variation: Use blue cheese or brie instead of goat cheese.

Stuffed Italian Mushrooms

This is a perfect appetizer to begin any meal.

20 large (2–2½ inches in diameter) white mushrooms (1 pound)

1½ cups Italian seasoned bread crumbs

4 tablespoons olive oil

2 cloves garlic, minced

½ cup plus 2 tablespoons finely grated Parmigiano Reggiano cheese

¼ cup finely chopped parsley

½ teaspoon dried oregano

2 tablespoons butter

½ teaspoon salt

¼ teaspoon pepper

Preheat oven to 400°F.

Wash mushrooms well under cold water and pat dry on paper towels. Pull stems from mushroom caps (to create space for stuffing) and finely chop stems. Put mushroom caps, stem side down, in a lightly oiled large shallow baking pan and bake in middle of oven until mushrooms exude liquid (about 10 minutes). Remove from oven.

While mushrooms are baking, combine bread crumbs, olive oil, garlic, ½ cup Parmigiano Reggiano cheese, parsley, and oregano and mix well. Heat butter in skillet over medium heat and sauté the chopped mushroom stems until all liquid is absorbed (about 5 minutes). Add mushroom stems to bread crumbs along with salt and pepper and mix well.

Turn mushroom caps over, then mound mushroom filling in caps, pressing gently (there will be some filling left over). Sprinkle remaining 2 tablespoons of Parmigiano Reggiano cheese over stuffed mushrooms and bake in middle of oven until mushrooms are tender and stuffing is golden brown (about 20 minutes).

The Lighter Side

Grilled Chicken Sandwiches with Sun-Dried Tomatoes and Goat Cheese Spread

The goat cheese spread adds a unique flavor to these grilled chicken sandwiches.

4 boneless skinless chicken breast halves, well trimmed

2 tablespoons balsamic vinegar

1 tablespoon lemon juice

2 tablespoons olive oil

2 cloves garlic, minced

2 teaspoons minced fresh rosemary

1 red onion, cut into ½-inch-thick slices

4 ounces soft goat cheese

½ cup chopped, drained, oil-packed sun-dried tomatoes

4 large onion rolls, cut in half

2 cups fresh spinach

Place chicken in medium bowl. Mix together the vinegar, lemon juice, olive oil, garlic, and rosemary. Cover and refrigerate chicken for at least 4 hours or overnight.

Prepare barbecue (medium-high heat) or heat your Foreman grill. Remove chicken from marinade and sprinkle with salt and pepper. Grill chicken and onion slices until chicken is just cooked through and onions are golden brown, turning occasionally (about 15 minutes). While chicken is cooking, mix together in a small bowl the goat cheese and sun-dried tomatoes.

Grill cut sides of rolls until golden brown. Spread bottom halves of rolls with goat cheese mixture. Top with chicken breast and some grilled onions and spinach. Spread top halves of rolls with more of the goat cheese and place atop sandwiches. Serves 4.

Variation: Omit the goat cheese and sun-dried tomatoes and grill chicken as directed above. Top each piece with 2 slices of crispy bacon and one slice of Swiss of cheese. Put lid on grill and cook until cheese melts or place under a broiler until cheese melts.

Rice Salad with Fresh Vegetables and Feta Cheese Dressing

The basmati rice makes this dish very light and perfect to take to a tailgating party.

Dressing

- ¾ cup olive oil
- ½ cup crumbled soft feta cheese
- ¼ cup plus 2 tablespoons red wine vinegar
- 2 tablespoons chopped fresh oregano (or 1 teaspoon dried oregano)
- 1 tablespoon ground cumin
- ½ teaspoon ground cloves

Combine all of the above ingredients in a large bowl and set aside.

Bring 4½ cups water to simmer in heavy large saucepan. Add rice and 1 teaspoon salt and stir to combine. Reduce heat to low, cover, and simmer until rice is cooked through (about 20 minutes). Remove from heat and let stand 5 minutes.

Salad

- 4½ cups water
- 2½ cups uncooked basmati rice
- 1 teaspoon salt
- 1 cup chopped celery
- 1 cup chopped green bell pepper
- 1 cup chopped red bell pepper
- 1 cup chopped red onion
- ½ cup chopped fresh chives
- 2 cups frozen corn, thawed and drained
- salt and pepper to taste

Transfer rice to large bowl. Fluff with fork. Pour cheese dressing over hot rice and let cool, tossing occasionally. Mix in celery, red and green bell peppers, onion, chives, and corn. Season with salt and pepper. Serves 8.

Patty Melt

Not only will vegetarians love these, so will your meat-eating friends.

2 beef patties, turkey patties, or vegi patties

4 slices rye bread

4 slices Monterey Jack cheese

½ onion, sliced

2 tablespoons butter

Follow recipes for turkey burgers or beef burgers or use Morningstar frozen vegi burgers. Cook burgers on the grill, in a Foreman grill, or in a skillet to preferred doneness. In another small skillet sauté onion in 2 tablespoons butter until soft and slightly brown. Butter one side of each slice of bread. Heat a skillet over medium heat. Add two slices of bread butter side down. Top each slice with one piece of cheese, a burger, onions, and another piece of cheese. Then place other piece of bread on top with buttered side up. Cook until nicely browned on one side; turn over and cook other side until nicely browned. Serves 2.

Low-fat variation: Use turkey or vegi patties; substitute light margarine for butter; use low-fat Monterey Jack cheese or provolone cheese.

White Chicken Chili

This is a delicious alternative to regular tomato-based chili.

4 tablespoons olive oil

1 large onion, chopped

2 poblano green peppers, sliced thin (can substitute green bell peppers)

2 cloves garlic, minced

2 cups shredded rotisserie chicken

2 tablespoons ground cumin

5 cups chicken broth

1 15-ounce can northern white beans, drained and rinsed

Heat olive oil in a large saucepan over medium heat. Add onion, peppers, and garlic. Cook until onion and peppers are soft (about 10 minutes). Add the chicken and cumin and stir well. Add the chicken broth and then the white beans. Stir well. Reduce heat and simmer for about 15 minutes. Serves 4.

Variation: Place all ingredients in a slow cooker and cook on low for 6 hours.

Entrées

Grilled Mahi-Mahi with Lemon Cream and Chives

This light and flavorful dish is perfect for fish lovers.

4 mahi-mahi fish fillets

2 tablespoons olive oil

Salt and pepper

½ stick (¼ cup) unsalted butter

2 large shallots

½ cup dry white wine

1 cup chicken or vegetable broth

2 tablespoons fresh lemon juice

¾ cup heavy cream

2 teaspoons finely grated fresh lemon zest

½ cup chopped fresh chives

Preheat the grill to medium-high heat or heat your Foreman grill. Place fish fillets on a platter and spread each fillet with olive oil, salt, and pepper. Set aside.

Meanwhile, make the lemon cream sauce. In a medium saucepan over medium heat melt butter, add the shallots, and sauté until soft (about 8 minutes). Add the white wine and chicken broth and cook until the mixture is reduced by half. Add the lemon juice, cream, and lemon zest and stir well. Reduce heat to low and simmer while you cook the mahi-mahi.

Place each fillet on the grill and cook for 5 minutes. Gently flip the fillets over and cook for another 4–5 minutes or until cooked through, depending on thickness of the fish. Place each fillet on a plate. Add chives to cream sauce and stir. Spoon a generous portion of sauce over each fillet and serve immediately. Serves 4.

Spanish Shrimp Scampi

This recipe is much easier than traditional scampi dishes and is exceptionally yummy.

16 large shrimp, peeled and deveined

½ cup olive oil

4 minced cloves garlic

½ teaspoon salt

¼ teaspoon pepper

¼ teaspoon red pepper flakes

chopped parsley for garnish (optional)

Preheat broiler.

Place olive oil in a shallow dish large enough to lay all the shrimp out, or you can divide olive oil in two and use two gratin dishes for individual servings. Heat oil under broiler until it sizzles. Working very quickly, add garlic to hot oil and immediately add shrimp, poking them around to make sure they are all lying in oil. If using two gratin dishes, divide garlic and shrimp between dishes. Broil for 3 minutes with oven door open. Stir gently and add salt and pepper. Continue broiling for additional 3 minutes or until shrimp is cooked through. Sprinkle with chopped parsley. Serve immediately. Serves 2.

Grandma's Southern Fried Chicken

You can eat this hot or make it a day ahead and take it to game day cold.

1 3–3½ pound fryer, cut into eight pieces

1½ cups buttermilk

1¾ teaspoons salt

1½ teaspoons pepper

½ teaspoon ground cumin

½ teaspoon cayenne pepper

2 cups unbleached all-purpose flour

2 cups solid vegetable shortening
(like Crisco)

Mix buttermilk, salt, pepper, cumin, and cayenne pepper in large bowl. Add chicken and turn to coat each piece. Cover and chill at least 3 hours or overnight. Mix flour with a little more salt and pepper. Remove chicken pieces from buttermilk and dip in the flour, turning to coat; shake off excess flour. Transfer chicken to rack on baking sheet. Let stand at least 15 minutes.

Preheat oven to 200°F. Line a baking sheet with paper towels and set aside.

Melt the shortening in a large heavy skillet to a depth of about ¾ inch. Heat oil to 375°F or until a small piece of bread sizzles instantly when added. Add chicken drumsticks and thighs first, reducing heat to medium low. Cover and cook until chicken is golden brown (about 13 minutes). Turn chicken over. Cook uncovered until that side browns. You may need to turn the chicken several times to cook evenly and prevent burning. Cooking time should be about 30 minutes total. When the chicken is about ready, turn up the heat again so that the chicken is very crisp and hot when removed from the skillet. Using tongs, take the chicken out and transfer to the paper towel–lined baking sheet. Put in oven to keep warm while you cook the rest of the chicken. With a strainer, remove any brown bits from the oil and discard. Then reheat the shortening to 375°F and repeat cooking method with the chicken breasts. Using tongs, transfer chicken to prepared sheet and drain. Serve hot or at room temperature or cold for tailgating. Serves 6.

Chicken Enchiladas in Salsa Verde

You don't need to go to a Mexican restaurant when you can make these in your own kitchen.

2 large cooked chicken breasts, shredded (can use a rotisserie chicken)

14 corn tortillas

2 tablespoons olive oil

2 cloves garlic, minced

3 15-ounce jars salsa verde

½ cup chicken broth

1 cup chopped cilantro

1½ cups sour cream

2 cups shredded Monterey Jack cheese

Preheat oven to 350°F. Lightly oil a 9- × 13-inch baking dish and set aside.

In a heavy nonstick skillet over medium high, toast one or two tortillas at a time on each side until slightly brown. Transfer to a plate and continue toasting all of the tortillas. Set aside.

In the same skillet, heat olive oil over medium heat. Add the garlic until it begins to sizzle and then pour in the salsa verde and the chicken broth. Cook the salsa for about 10 minutes. Turn off the heat, add the cilantro, and stir.

Using a cutting board as a work surface, dip each tortilla in the salsa, place on cutting board, and spread about 1 tablespoon of shredded chicken at one end of tortilla. Roll up and place in prepared baking dish. Continue process until all tortillas are used. Pour the remaining salsa verde over enchiladas. Spread the sour cream over the salsa and sprinkle with cheese. Bake for 30 minutes until sauce is bubbling and cheese begins to brown. Serves 4–5.

Low-fat variation: Substitute fat-free sour cream for regular sour cream; low-fat Monterey Jack cheese for regular Monterey cheese.

Chicken Stuffed with Goat Cheese in Mushroom Marsala Sauce

This elegant chicken dish will have your friends convinced you're a gourmet cook.

4 boneless chicken breast halves

6 ounces soft goat cheese

½ cup chopped basil

½ cup chopped fresh chives

1 egg, beaten

1½ cups Italian seasoned bread crumbs

1 cup white cooking wine

½ stick (¼ cup) butter

3 cloves garlic, minced

2 pounds mushrooms, sliced

2 cups Marsala (sweet) wine (found in the wine section by the ports; cooking sherry would work as a substitute)

Preheat oven to 350°F. Lightly oil a 9- × 11-inch baking dish and set aside.

Place a strip of parchment paper on a cutting board and pound the chicken breasts with a meat mallet to flatten.

In a medium bowl mix together the goat cheese, basil, and chives. Place a mound of the goat cheese mixture at the end of each chicken breast, roll up, and secure with toothpicks. Use enough toothpicks to close any openings and to make sure cheese doesn't seep out while cooking.

Once you've rolled all four chicken breasts, place bread crumbs on a plate and dip each piece of chicken in the beaten egg mixture and then the bread crumbs to coat all the way around. Place in prepared baking dish. Pour wine into dish and cover chicken with foil and bake for 15 minutes. Remove foil after 15 minutes and continue cooking for another 15 minutes or until a thermometer inserted into chicken registers 170°F.

While chicken is baking, make the mushroom sauce. Heat butter in a large skillet over medium-high heat. Add the garlic until it begins to sizzle; add mushrooms and stir well. Continue cooking mushrooms until all liquid has evaporated and they begin to brown (about 15 to 20 minutes). Turn heat to high; add the Marsala wine and stir well. Continue cooking until wine is reduced slightly and sauce begins to thicken. Place a chicken breast on a plate and pour a generous serving of the mushroom sauce over and repeat with other 3 pieces. Serves 4.

French-Style Beef Bourguignon

Who knew beef stew could be this good? The time this recipe takes is well worth it.

3 pounds boneless beef chuck, cut into 2-inch pieces

⅓ cup all-purpose flour

3 tablespoons olive oil

5 large cloves garlic, minced

½ cup brandy

4½ tablespoons unsalted butter

2 onions, finely chopped

4 carrots, cut into ¼-inch-thick slices

½ cup parsley chopped

2 tablespoons fresh thyme sprigs, chopped

1 tablespoon fresh rosemary, chopped

2 bay leaves

1 tablespoon tomato paste

1 (750-ml) bottle dry red wine (preferably Burgundy or Côtes du Rhône)

1 pound mushrooms, quartered if large

1 teaspoon salt

½ teaspoon pepper

Divide flour and beef between two large sealable bags and shake well to coat beef. In a large heavy skillet, heat 2 tablespoons olive oil over medium-high heat. Add 2 cloves of the minced garlic and one bag of the beef and brown on all sides. Place in a bowl. Add another tablespoon of oil for second batch and another 2 cloves of garlic and brown second batch of beef. Pour the first batch back in with second batch of meat and heat up. Add brandy to the meat and ignite with a lighter (be careful not to stand too close). Wait for flames to subside. Transfer meat to a bowl and set aside. In the same skillet melt the butter over medium-high heat and add remaining garlic, onions, and carrots and cook for 8 minutes. Add parsley, thyme, rosemary, and bay leaves and stir until fragrant. Add tomato paste and stir well. Add wine, meat with juices and mushrooms, salt, and pepper and cook for 3½ to 4 hours until thick. Correct seasoning with salt and pepper if needed. Serves 8.

Variation: After you brown the meat, add the brandy and let it cook off. Then place in a slow cooker with remaining ingredients and cook for about 6 hours.

Grilled Pork Kabobs with Chimichurri Sauce

If you love Brazilian churrascaria, this dish will do just fine.

1 1½-pound pork tenderloin, cut into thick pieces

Olive oil

2 tablespoons dark brown sugar

1 tablespoon sweet smoked paprika

1 tablespoon coarse kosher salt

1½ teaspoons chipotle or ancho chili powder

1 teaspoon ground black pepper

Soak 4 wooden skewers in cold water for 15 minutes. Once you cut pork into pieces, pat dry with paper towels.

Combine all spice ingredients in a bowl and mix well. Drizzle pork with olive oil and dip each piece in the spice rub. Place on skewer. Repeat with remaining pork until all the meat is skewered.

Prepare the grill by heating to medium-high. Grill the pork on one side for about 8–10 minutes until pork is brown. Turn over and continue cooking until done (about another 15 minutes), turning as needed so that pork does not burn. Serve with chimichurri dipping sauce. Serves 4.

Variation: Alternate pieces of red bell pepper and onion between the meat.

Chimichurri Sauce

¾ cup olive oil

2 tablespoons sherry wine vinegar or red wine vinegar

2 tablespoons fresh lemon juice

2 cloves garlic, peeled

1 medium shallot, peeled, quartered

1 teaspoon fine sea salt

½ teaspoon freshly ground black pepper

½ teaspoon dried crushed red pepper

½ cup stemmed fresh oregano

1½ cups (packed) stemmed fresh parsley

1 cup (packed) stemmed fresh cilantro
   or basil (whichever you prefer)

Puree all ingredients in processor. Transfer to bowl. Add remaining olive oil. (Can be made 2 hours ahead. Cover and let stand at room temperature.)

Variation: Substitute dried herbs, 2 teaspoons each, for fresh oregano, parsley, and cilantro or basil.

Three-Cheese Lasagna with Spinach

This lasagna can be made with meat sauce as well.

Sauce

2 tablespoons olive oil

1 cup chopped onion

2 cloves garlic, minced

1 28-ounce can crushed tomatoes

2 cups tomato sauce

1 small can tomato paste

¼ cup chopped fresh basil (or 2 teaspoons dried)

1 tablespoon golden brown sugar

2 teaspoons dried oregano

2 teaspoons dried basil

1 bay leaf

½ teaspoon dried crushed red pepper

Heat oil in heavy large saucepan over medium heat. Add onion and garlic and sauté until softened (about 12 minutes). Add remaining ingredients. Cover and simmer, stirring occasionally, until flavors blend and sauce measures about 5 cups (about 15 minutes). Discard bay leaf and cool. The sauce can be made a day ahead. Just cool, cover, and refrigerate.

For Lasagna

18 lasagna noodles

2 15-ounce containers part-skim ricotta cheese

1½ cups grated Parmesan cheese

1 10-ounce package frozen chopped spinach, thawed, drained, and squeezed dry (optional)

2 large eggs, beaten

Salt and pepper

3¾ cups grated mozzarella cheese

Preheat oven to 350°F.

You can use the lasagna noodles that don't require preboiling or regular noodles. If using regular lasagna noodles, cook in large pot of boiling salted water until almost tender (about 7 minutes). Drain and cover with cold water.

In a large bowl, combine the ricotta cheese, ¾ cup Parmesan, spinach, and eggs. Mix well. Add salt and pepper to taste.

Spread ½ cup sauce over bottom of 13- × 9-inch glass baking dish. Place 6 noodles over sauce, overlapping to fit. Spread half of ricotta-spinach mixture evenly over noodles. Sprinkle 1½ cups mozzarella cheese evenly over ricotta-spinach mixture. Spoon enough sauce over cheese to cover (about 1½ cups), spreading with spatula. Repeat layering with 6 noodles, remaining ricotta-spinach mixture, 1½ cups mozzarella, and 1½ cups sauce. Arrange remaining 6 noodles over sauce. Spread remaining sauce over noodles. Sprinkle remaining ¾ cup mozzarella cheese and ¾ cup Parmesan cheese evenly over lasagna. Cover baking dish with aluminum foil. Bake lasagna 40 minutes; uncover and bake until hot and bubbly (about 30 minutes). Let lasagna stand 15 minutes before serving. Serves 10.

Note: Lasagna can be prepared up to 1 day ahead. Cover tightly with plastic wrap and refrigerate; freeze what you don't eat.

Variation: For meat lovers, use Bolognese sauce from the Junior chapter (see page 79).

Sides

Tortilla Española (Spanish potato frittata)

This is a delicious Spanish dish I learned how to make when I lived in Madrid. You can serve it as an appetizer, put it in sandwiches, or serve as an accompaniment to just about any entrée.

5 eggs, beaten

½ cup plus 2 tablespoons olive oil

3 large russet potatoes, peeled and sliced

1 large onion, sliced

1 teaspoon salt

½ teaspoon pepper

Beat eggs in a large bowl and set aside. Heat ½ cup olive oil in a heavy nonstick skillet over medium-high heat. Add ⅓ of the potatoes, ⅓ of the onion, and repeat, making 3 layers. Cover potatoes and cook for about 5 to 8 minutes until they begin to brown on the bottom. Then turn with a spatula. Mixture will not remain in layers, but that's okay. Continue cooking the potatoes, turning as needed so that they can brown but not burn. Keep a lid on them between turnings so that potatoes will cook evenly. Once potatoes are cooked completely (about 20 to 25 minutes), set a strainer in the sink and pour the potatoes into the strainer. Let potatoes rest for 5 minutes.

Pour potatoes into the beaten egg mixture, add salt and pepper, and stir well. The mixture will be very moist. Clean the skillet you just used or use a different one and heat 1 tablespoon of oil in it over medium-high heat. Once oil is hot, pour potato mixture in and smooth over with a spatula. Let the tortilla cook on one side for about 4 to 5 minutes, shaking the pan every so often so it doesn't stick. Using a large plate that covers the skillet, turn the tortilla onto the plate. Place a little more oil in the pan and carefully slide the tortilla back into the skillet, using a spatula to assist you, and cook the other side of the tortilla for an additional 4 to 5 minutes, shaking the pan to prevent sticking. Once the tortilla is a nice golden brown, turn off the heat and, using the same plate, invert the tortilla onto the plate. Sprinkle with salt and pepper and cut into wedges. Serves 8.

Variation: In Spain, they slice this tortilla and place it on a toasted baguette. First follow the instructions for Pan con Tomate in the Freshman chapter (see page 7) and then simply add slices of this tortilla to it. Delicious!

Goat Cheese Scalloped Potatoes

These rich, creamy potatoes go well with roasted meats.

½ (¼ cup) stick butter

½ cup chopped onion

2 cloves garlic, minced

¾ cup dry white wine

1½ cups heavy cream

1¼ cups canned chicken broth

3 teaspoons herbes de Provence (a dried
herb mixture available in specialty stores
and some supermarkets; if unavailable,
substitute ½ teaspoon thyme, ½ teaspoon
sage, and ½ teaspoon rosemary)

1 teaspoon salt

½ teaspoon pepper

1 10½- to 11-ounce log soft fresh goat cheese,
crumbled

6 russet potatoes, peeled and thinly sliced

Preheat oven to 400°F. Butter a 13- × 9-inch glass baking dish.

Melt butter in a large pot over medium-high heat. Add the onion and garlic and cook for about 5 minutes. Add the wine and simmer for 2 minutes. Add the cream, chicken broth, herbes de Provence, salt, and pepper and bring liquid to simmer. Add half the cheese and whisk until smooth. Put remaining cheese in the fridge to chill. Add the potatoes to the pot and bring to simmer.

Transfer potato mixture to prepared dish, spreading evenly. Cover with foil; bake 15 minutes. Uncover and bake until potatoes are very tender and liquid bubbles thickly (about 50 minutes).

Dot potatoes with remaining cheese. Bake until cheese begins to brown on top (about 5 minutes). Let cool 15 minutes before serving. Serves 8.

Zucchini-Tomato Gratin

This yummy side dish is easy to prepare and oh-so good.

2 large zucchini, sliced lengthwise in thin strips

4 large tomatoes, sliced and seeds removed

Salt

2 cups Italian seasoned bread crumbs

2 cloves garlic, minced

½ cup Parmesan cheese plus 2 tablespoons

½ cup olive oil

Preheat oven to 350°F. Lightly grease with olive oil a 9- × 13-inch glass baking dish.

Spread out zucchini and tomatoes on paper towels and lightly salt them to bring out the excess liquid. Let them stand for about 15–20 minutes.

Meanwhile, place bread crumbs, garlic, ½ cup cheese, and olive oil in a medium bowl and mix well. Pat tomatoes and zucchini dry with paper towels. Put a layer of zucchini on bottom, then a layer of tomatoes. Sprinkle with ½ of the bread crumb mixture and repeat a second layer, ending with remaining bread crumb mixture sprinkled over the top followed by 2 tablespoons of cheese. Bake for 30 minutes. Serves 8.

Creamy Corn Salad

This salad is great for a barbeque.

3 cans whole-kernel white sweet corn, drained

1 cucumber, diced

1 tomato, seeded and diced

½ cup diced onion

1 cup sour cream

1½ tablespoons red wine vinegar

½ teaspoon celery seed

½ teaspoon salt

¼ teaspoon pepper

Mix the corn, cucumber, tomato, and onion in a medium bowl. In a separate small bowl whisk together the sour cream, vinegar, celery seed, salt, and pepper. Pour sour cream over the corn and spread like icing: do not mix. Place in refrigerator for at least 1 hour. When ready to serve, mix the sour cream topping into the corn and gently stir. Serves 6.

Braised Brussels Sprouts

Braising takes the bitterness out of brussels sprouts, and even those who don't like this vegetable may find themselves asking for seconds.

10 brussels sprouts, end and outer layer removed, cut in half from top to bottom

2 tablespoons olive oil

2 cloves garlic, minced

2 teaspoons sugar

Salt and pepper

Clean brussels sprouts. Put a cup of water in a medium pot and place a steamer basket inside with the sprouts; cover with a lid. Turn heat to high and steam brussels sprouts for about 4 minutes. Pour sprouts into a colander and rinse under cold water to stop cooking and retain color.

Heat olive oil in a large skillet over medium-high heat. Add the garlic until it begins to sizzle; then add sugar and stir. Add brussels sprouts to skillet and cook until sprouts begin to braise and are tender, stirring occasionally (about 6 minutes). Sprinkle with salt and pepper to taste. Serves 4.

Desserts

Super-Moist Chocolate Sheet Cake

This no-fail moist cake will satisfy that chocolate craving.

1 cup coffee or you can use water

1½ sticks unsalted butter, room temperature

¾ cup unsweetened cocoa powder

½ cup vegetable oil

1 teaspoon vanilla extract

1 teaspoon baking soda

2 cups sugar

2 cups all-purpose flour

½ teaspoon salt

½ cup buttermilk

2 large eggs, beaten

Frosting

1 stick butter

4½ tablespoons whole milk

3 tablespoons unsweetened cocoa powder

4 cups powdered sugar

1 teaspoon vanilla extract

1 cup chopped pecans or walnuts

Preheat oven to 350°F. Butter and flour 15½- × 9½- × 1-inch baking sheet pan.

Whisk together coffee or water, butter, cocoa powder, vegetable oil, 1 teaspoon vanilla, and baking soda in large bowl to mix well. Whisk in sugar, flour, and salt; then add buttermilk and eggs. Spread batter in prepared baking sheet. Bake cake until tester inserted into center comes out clean (about 20 minutes). Transfer cake in pan to rack.

To make frosting, melt butter with the milk and powdered cocoa in heavy medium saucepan. Bring to boil over medium heat. Remove from heat. Whisk in powdered sugar, vanilla, and nuts.

Spread frosting over warm cake. Cool cake completely in pan. Cut into 24 pieces. To store cake, cover with foil and refrigerate, or if planning to eat the cake within a couple of days, cover and store at room temperature. You can also freeze this cake.

White Chocolate Cheesecake

This was my best-selling cheesecake when I worked as a caterer. Try it and you'll see why.

Crust

2½ cups graham cracker crumbs

¼ cup sugar

1 stick butter, melted

Filling

5 8-ounce packages cream cheese, softened
   (use light cream cheese if you want to reduce calories)

3 tablespoons flour

1¾ cups sugar

5 eggs, room temperature

2 teaspoons vanilla

¼ cup heavy cream

1 cup white chocolate, chopped

Topping

1½ cups sour cream

¼ cup sugar

½ teaspoon vanilla

1½ cups white chocolate, chopped or grated

Preheat oven to 300°F.

In a 9-inch springform pan, mix together the graham crackers and sugar. Then add the melted butter. Press the crumb mixture to bottom and up the sides of the pan about ¼ inch. Set aside.

For filling, use an electric mixer to beat the cream cheese in a large mixing bowl until it is soft. Scrape down the sides of the bowl with a spatula to make sure all the cream cheese is softened. Add the flour and sugar and beat for about 2 to 3 minutes until fluffy. With mixer running, begin adding eggs one at time, mixing after each one. Once all eggs are incorporated, turn off mixer and, using a spatula, fold in the vanilla, cream, and white chocolate. Pour mixture into prepared crust and bake for 1 hour 15 minutes. Turn off the oven and let cake sit in oven for another 10 minutes. Run a knife around the edge of cake and let it cool completely.

Once the cake is cool, refrigerate it for at least 5 hours or overnight. When ready to serve, run a knife under hot water and then around edges of cake to loosen. Remove the sides of springform pan. For topping, in a small bowl, mix together the sour cream, sugar, and vanilla and spread over the top of the cake. Sprinkle with the white chocolate and serve. Serves 12.

Low-fat/reduced-calorie variation: Use light margarine instead of butter; light cream cheese; low-fat sour cream; substitute Splenda for the sugar.

Mom's Apple Pie

Using the optional ready-made piecrusts won't take away from this pie's flavor.

crust (or use ready-made piecrusts)

2½ cups unbleached all-purpose flour

¼ cup sugar

1 teaspoon salt

1 teaspoon apple pie spice

1 stick chilled unsalted butter, cut into pieces

⅓ cup chilled solid vegetable shortening

7 tablespoons sour cream

Mix flour, sugar, salt, and apple pie spice in large mixing bowl. Using a fork or pastry cutter, add butter and shortening and cut in until mixture resembles coarse meal. (This can also be done in a food processor.) Add sour cream and blend together until a soft dough forms. If using a processor, use on/off turns just until dough forms. Turn out dough onto lightly floured surface. Divide in half. Form each half into a ball; flatten into disk. Wrap each disk in plastic and refrigerate 1 hour.

Filling

6 Gala or Granny Smith apples, peeled,
   cored, and sliced

2 tablespoons lemon juice

2 tablespoons cornstarch or flour

2 teaspoons cinnamon

¼ cup apple juice

½ cup brown sugar, packed

4 tablespoons light butter at room temperature

Preheat oven to 350°F.

In a large bowl mix together apples, lemon juice, cornstarch, and cinnamon. Add remaining ingredients and stir well.

On a cutting board covered with plastic, roll out half of the piecrust. Place crust in a 9-inch pie pan and fill with apple mixture. Roll out the second crust and drape over filled pie shell.

Trim overlapping edges with a sharp knife. Crimp edges to fasten to bottom crust to seal. Cut 5 slashes in top of dough to allow steam to escape. If you prefer the lattice look for your crust, you can cut eight ½-inch-thick strips from the second crust and lay them in a crisscross pattern on top of the apples. Bake 55 minutes or until golden brown. Sprinkle top with cinnamon. Serves 8.

Let's Do Some Tailgating

Tailgating Menu 1

As You Like It—Mexican Salsa and Chips	5
Southwest Beef or Turkey Burgers	13
Black Bean Veggie Burgers	41
Creamy Corn Salad	118
Chocolate No-Bake Cookies	26

Tailgating Menu 2

Citrus-Marinated Shrimp	69
Grilled Pork Kabobs with Chimichurri Sauce	110
Tortilla Española (Spanish potato fritter)	114
Chopped Salad Your Way	8
Decadent Chocolate Brownies	56

Tailgating Menu 3

As You Like It—Mexican Salsa and Chips	5
Stadium Chili	72
Oriental Coleslaw	36
Mom's Apple Pie	124

Tailgating Menu 4

Spinach and Mushroom Frittata	96
Crunchy Chicken Salad	40
Cavender's Pasta Salad	12
Chocolate Peanut Butter Balls	59

Tailgating Menu 5

Turkey Wraps	10
Vegetarian Chili	42
Rice Salad with Fresh Vegetables and Feta Cheese Dressing	101
Dreamy Lemon Bars	60

Tailgating Menu 6

Key Lime Shrimp on the Grill	43
Grandma's Southern Fried Chicken	106
Dilled Potato Salad	52
Super-Moist Chocolate Sheet Cake	120

Tailgating Menu 7

Grilled Chicken Sandwiches with Sun-Dried Tomatoes and Goat Cheese Spread	100
Curried Couscous with Veggies	50
Key Lime Pie	88

Tailgating Menu 8

Tortilla Española (Spanish potato fritter)	114
Philly Cheese Steak Sandwiches	73
Chopped Salad Your Way	8
Grandma's Blueberry-Apple Crisp	90

Tailgating Menu 9

As You Like It—Mexican Salsa and Chips	5
White Chicken Chili	103
Sweet Southern Cornbread	87
Apple Cake with Vanilla Sauce	58

Tailgating Menu 10

Grilled Southwest Chicken with Black Bean Salsa	19
Pan con Tomate	7
Rice Salad with Fresh Vegetables and Feta Cheese Dressing	101
Decadent Chocolate Brownies	56

Tailgating Menu 11: Breakfast/Brunch

Blueberry Muffins	62
Banana Nut Bread with Chocolate Chips	94
Easy Quiche Lorraine	70
Healthy Fruit Salad	9
Chocolate No-Bake Cookies	26

Tailgating Menu 12: Breakfast/Brunch

Spinach and Mushroom Frittata	96
Tortilla Española (Spanish potato fritter)	114
Caprese Salad	35
Chocolate-Dipped Strawberries	27

Essential and Nonessential Items to Take to College

VEGETABLES ARE COOL, MAN

Essentials

Basting brush
Blender
Colander
Cutting boards
Garlic press
Handheld juicer
Handheld lemon zester
Hand mixer
Heavy-duty sauce spoons
Kitchen string
Knives: paring, bread, steak, chopping
Loaf pan
Measuring cups
Meat mallet
Meat and candy thermometers
Mixing bowls
Muffin pan
Pizza cutter
Plastic containers

Potato masher
Potato peeler
Pots and pans
Rubber spatulas
Skewers
Skillet, nonstick
Springform pan
Steamer basket
Tongs
Whisk
Wooden spoons

Nonessentials

Food processor
Foreman grill
Handheld pastry cutter
Slow cooker (crockpot)
Toaster oven

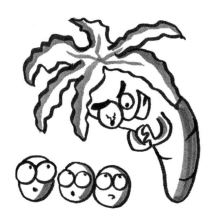

Pantry Items to Take to College

The following list is a good base of seasonings to have on hand:

Baking powder

Basil

Black pepper

Cayenne pepper

Chili powder

Chives

Cinnamon

Cumin

Curry powder

Dill

Flour

Garlic (fresh)

KC Masterpiece seasoning
for chicken and beef

Oregano

Paprika

Red pepper flakes, crushed

Rosemary

Salt

Seasoned salt

Thyme

Sugar, white, brown, and powdered

Vanilla extract

Essential Condiments and Wraps

Aluminum foil

Balsamic vinegar

Bouillon, chicken,
beef, and vegetable

Italian seasoned
bread crumbs

Ketchup

Mayonnaise

Mustard—Dijon and yellow

Olive oil

Pancake syrup

Parchment paper

Plastic wrap

Red wine vinegar

Soy sauce

Tabasco sauce

White cooking wine

Worchester sauce

Glossary of Cooking Terms

Al dente: "to the tooth," in Italian. The pasta is cooked just enough to maintain a firm, chewy texture. Boil pasta according to package instructions at the minimum cooking time indicated on the package or even a minute before. Take a piece out and run under cold water to test. If pasta is mildly chewy but doesn't stick to your teeth, it's al dente. If it sticks to your teeth, cook a minute longer and retest.

Baste: to brush or spoon liquid fat or juices over meat during roasting to add flavor and to prevent it from drying out.

Beat: to smoothen a mixture by briskly whipping or stirring it with a spoon, fork, wire whisk, rotary beater, or electric mixer.

Blanch: to boil briefly to loosen the skin of a fruit or a vegetable. After 30 seconds in boiling water, the fruit or vegetable should be plunged into ice water to stop the cooking action, and then the skin easily slides off.

Blend: to mix or fold two or more ingredients together to obtain equal distribution throughout the mixture.

Boil: to cook food in heated water or other liquid that is bubbling vigorously.

Boiling eggs: Place egg or eggs in a saucepan, run cold water over to cover about an inch above egg, place on stove, and cook over medium-high heat until water boils. Reduce heat to low and simmer 2–3 minutes for soft-boiled eggs and

12–15 minutes for hard-boiled egg. Place pan in sink and run cold water over until egg is cool. Gently tap egg on hard surface and peel under cold water.

Braising: a cooking technique that requires browning meat in oil or other fat and then cooking slowly in liquid. The effect of braising is to tenderize the meat and retain the juices.

Bread: to coat the food with crumbs (usually with soft or dry bread crumbs), sometimes seasoned.

Broil: to cook food directly under the heat source.

Broth or stock: a flavorful liquid made by gently cooking meat, seafood, or vegetables (and/or their by-products, such as bones and trimming), often with herbs, in liquid, usually water.

Browning: a quick sautéing, pan/oven broiling, or grilling method done either at the beginning or end of meal preparation, often to enhance flavor, texture, or eye appeal.

Butterfly: to cut open a food such as shrimp or pork chops down the center without cutting all the way through, and then spread apart.

Caramelization: browning sugar over a flame, with or without the addition of some water to aid the process. The temperature range in which sugar caramelizes is approximately 320°F to 360°F.

Chop: to cut into irregular pieces.

Clarify: to remove impurities from butter or stock by heating the liquid, then straining or skimming it.

Coddle: to cook in liquid just below the boiling point.

Combine: to blend two or more ingredients into a single mixture.

Confit: to cook pieces of meat slowly in their own gently rendered fat.

Core: to remove the inedible center of fruits such as pineapples.

Cream: to beat vegetable shortening, butter, or margarine, with or without sugar, until light and fluffy. This process traps in air bubbles, which create height in cookies and cakes.

Crimp: to create a decorative edge on a piecrust. On a double piecrust, this also seals the edges together.

Crisp: to restore the crunch to foods; vegetables such as celery and carrots can be crisped with an ice water bath, and foods such as stale crackers can be heated in a medium oven.

Crush: to condense a food to its smallest particles, usually using a mortar and pestle or a rolling pin.

Custard: a mixture of beaten egg, milk, and possibly other ingredients such as sweet or savory flavorings, which is cooked with gentle heat, often in a water bath or double boiler. As pie filling, the custard is frequently cooked and chilled before being layered into a prebaked crust.

Cut in: to work vegetable shortening, margarine, or butter into dry ingredients.

Dash: a measure approximately equal to 1/16 teaspoon.

Deep-fry: to completely submerge the food in hot oil.

Deglaze: to add liquid to a pan in which foods have been fried or roasted, in order to dissolve the caramelized juices stuck to the bottom of the pan.

Devein: to remove the blackish-gray vein from the back of a shrimp. The vein can be removed with a utensil called a deveiner or with the tip of a sharp knife. Small and medium shrimp need deveining for aesthetic purposes only. However, because the veins in large shrimp contain grit, they should always be removed.

Dice: to cut into cubes.

Direct heat: a cooking method that allows heat to meet food directly, such as grilling, broiling, or toasting.

Dot: to sprinkle food with small bits of an ingredient such as butter to allow for even melting.

Dredge: to sprinkle lightly and evenly with sugar or flour. A dredger has holes pierced in the lid to sprinkle evenly.

Drippings: the liquids left in the bottom of a roasting or frying pan after meat is cooked; used for making gravies and sauces.

Drizzle: to pour a liquid such as a sweet glaze or melted butter in a slow, light trickle over food.

Dust: to sprinkle food lightly with spices, sugar, or flour for a light coating.

Egg wash: a mixture of beaten eggs (yolks, whites, or whole eggs) with either milk or water. Used to coat cookies and other baked goods to give them a shine when baked.

Entrée: a French term that originally referred to the first course of a meal, served after the soup and before the meat courses. In the United States, it refers to the main dish of a meal.

Fillet: to remove the bones from meat or fish for cooking.

Flambé: to ignite a sauce or other liquid so that it flames.

Fold: to cut and mix lightly with a spoon to keep as much air in the mixture as possible.

Fry: to cook food in hot oil, usually until a crisp brown crust forms.

Garlic clove: Garlic is found in produce sections. A clove from a garlic bulb can be broken off with your fingers. To peel, place clove on a work surface, mash with outer edge of large knife, and peel away skin.

Garnish: a decorative piece of an edible ingredient such as parsley, lemon wedges, lime zest, croutons, or chocolate curls placed as a finishing touch on dishes or drinks.

Glaze: a liquid that gives an item a shiny surface. Examples are fruit jams that have been heated or chocolate thinned with melted vegetable shortening. Also, to cover a food with such a liquid.

Grate: to shred or cut down a food into fine pieces by rubbing it against a rough surface.

Gratin: to bind together or combine food with a liquid such as cream, milk, béchamel sauce, or tomato sauce, in a shallow dish. The mixture is then baked until cooked and set.

Grease: to coat a pan or skillet with a thin layer of oil.

Grill: to cook over the heat source (traditionally over wood coals) in the open air.

Grind: to mechanically cut a food into small pieces.

Hard-ball stage: in candy making, the point at which syrup has cooked long enough to form a solid ball in cold water.

Hull (also husk): to remove the leafy parts of soft fruits, such as strawberries or blackberries.

Ice: to cool cooked food by placing in ice; also, to spread frosting on a cake.

Jell: to become gelatinous, firm, or congealed.

Julienne: to cut into long thin strips.

Jus: the natural juices released by roasting meats.

Knead: to work dough with the heels of your hands in a pressing and folding motion until it becomes smooth and elastic.

Line: to place layers of edible (cake or bread slices) or inedible (foil or wax paper) ingredients in a pan to provide structure for a dish or to prevent sticking.

Marble: to gently swirl one food into another.

Marinate: to combine food with aromatic ingredients to add flavor.

Mash: to beat or press a food to remove lumps and make a smooth mixture.

Mix: to beat or stir two or more foods together until they are thoroughly combined.

Moisten: to add enough liquid to dry ingredients to dampen but not soak them.

Pan-broil: to cook a food in a skillet without added fat, removing any fat as it accumulates.

Panfry: to cook in a hot pan with small amount of hot oil, butter, or other fat, turning the food over once or twice.

Parboil: to partially cook in a boiling liquid.

Parchment: a heavy, heat-resistant paper used in cooking.

Pare: to peel or trim a food, usually vegetables.

Peaks: the mounds made in a mixture; for example, egg white that has been whipped to stiffness. Peaks are "stiff" if they stay upright, or "soft" if they curl over.

Pipe: to force a semisoft food through a bag (either a pastry bag or a plastic bag with one corner cut off) to decorate food.

Poach: to simmer in liquid.

Puree: to mash, blend, or sieve food into a thick liquid.

Ramekin: a small baking dish used for individual servings of sweet and savory dishes.

Reduce: to cook liquids down so that some of the water evaporates.

Refresh: to pour cold water over freshly cooked vegetables to prevent further cooking and retain color.

Render: to melt fat to make drippings.

Roast: to cook uncovered in the oven.

Roux: a cooked paste usually made from flour and butter and used to thicken sauces. To make a roux for gravy, use equal parts butter or oil and equal parts flour. For every tablespoon of flour used you will need 1 cup of liquid or broth. For example, for brown gravy, heat 2 tablespoons butter over medium heat and whisk in 2 tablespoons flour until a thick paste forms. Then slowly add, whisking constantly, 2 cups of beef broth. Cook until thickened.

Sauté: to cook food quickly in a small amount of oil in a skillet or sauté pan over direct heat. You can use any kind of meat you like and dredge in flour or not. Simply heat a little oil in a skillet and add the meat and cook on one side until brown; turn and cook the other side until meat is cooked through.

Scald: to heat a liquid such as milk to just below the boiling point; also to loosen the skin of fruits or vegetables by dipping them in boiling water.

Score: to tenderize meat by making a number of shallow (often diagonal) cuts across its surface. This technique is also useful in marinating, as it allows for better absorption of the marinade.

Sear: to seal in a meat's juices by cooking it quickly over very high heat.

Season: to enhance the flavor of foods by adding ingredients such as salt, pepper, oregano, basil, cinnamon, and a variety of other herbs, spices, condiments, and vinegars. Also, to treat a pot or pan (usually cast iron) with a coating of cooking oil and baking it in a 350°F oven for approximately 1 hour; this process seals any tiny rough spots on the pan's surface that may cause food to stick.

Set: to let food become solid. (See also "Jell.")

Shred: to cut or tear into long narrow strips, either by hand or by using a grater or food processor.

Sift: to remove large lumps from a dry ingredient such as flour or confectioners' sugar by passing it through a fine mesh. This process also incorporates air into the ingredients, making them lighter.

Simmer: to cook food in a liquid at a low enough temperature that small bubbles begin to break the surface.

Skewer: to cut any kind of meat into large chunks. Marinate if you like. If using wooden skewers, soak them in cold water for 15 minutes before you skewer the meat. Take one piece of meat and pierce the meat, pushing it to the opposite end but leaving enough room to pick up so that you can turn while grilling. Continue with rest of meat, leaving an inch on the bottom so that meat doesn't fall off the skewer.

Skim: to remove the top layer of fat from stocks, soups, sauces, or other liquids such as cream from milk.

Springform pan: a two-piece baking pan in which a spring-loaded collar fits around a base; the collar is removed after baking is complete. Used for foods that may be difficult to remove from regular pans, such as cheesecake.

Steam: to cook over boiling water in a covered pan. This method retains the shape, texture, and nutritional value of food better than methods such as boiling.

Steep: to soak dry ingredients (tea leaves, ground coffee, herbs, spices, etc.) in liquid until the flavor is infused into the liquid.

Stir-fry: to fast-fry small pieces of meat and vegetables over very high heat with continual and rapid stirring.

Thin: to reduce a mixture's thickness with the addition of more liquid.

Toss: to combine several ingredients thoroughly by mixing lightly.

Truss: to use string, skewers, or pins to hold together a food to maintain its shape while it cooks (usually applied to meat or poultry).

Vinaigrette: a general term referring to any sauce made with vinegar, oil, and seasonings.

Water bath: a gentle cooking technique in which a container is set in a pan of simmering water. (See also "Coddle.")

Whip: to incorporate air into ingredients such as cream or egg whites by beating until light and fluffy; also refers to the utensil used for this action. To whip cream, use heavy cream found in the dairy case at the grocer. Chill thoroughly. Pour cream into a mixing bowl. Add a little sugar if you want sweet whipped cream. Beat the cream with a hand mixer or electric mixer until soft peaks form. If you beat the mixture too much, it will turn into butter, so watch carefully during the mixing process. Chill.

Whisk: to mix or fluff by beating; also refers to the utensil used for this action.

Zest: the thin, brightly colored outer part of the rind of citrus fruits. It contains volatile oils, used as a flavoring.

Glossary of College Slang

All-nighter: an all-night study session.

All over it: to be on top of things or have everything under control; example: "I'm all over it, dude."

Alpha Greek: the male or female who "rules" the school Greek system—or thinks they do.

Antler festival: a party where the men out number the women.

Bag monsters: students who stay in bed all day.

Barney: British term for an unattractive male.

Betty: an attractive female.

Bio-hazard: a dorm room that hasn't been cleaned since school started.

Borrow the porcelain: to go to the bathroom.

Bunk: bad, false.

Cancer stick: a cigarette.

Cash cow: an ATM; example: "Gotta go to the cash cow before we head out."

Chill: calm down, relax.

Cold: hurtful, unfeeling, someone does you wrong; example: "That's cold, dude."

Crucial: cool, awesome, excellent.

Crushing: to have a little crush on someone.

Debo: to borrow without asking

Demics: short for "academics"; what you came to school for.

Digits: telephone number.

Dime: something or someone perfect.

Fat juice: any high-calorie soft drink.

Frosh: highly motivated freshman.

Fifteen-minute rule: "When the professor is fifteen minutes late we get to leave class."

FLWs: famous last words.

For serious?: an expression of doubt or surprise.

Fratastic: overly preppy or conceited.

Freshasaurus: a freshman who is clueless.

Frontload: eating and drinking before a party.

G2G: gots to go.

Gank: to steal.

Geck: an annoying person (from "gecko").

Hallcest: going out with person from your hall or dorm.

Horizontal engineering: napping.

Leet: cool, awesome, great (from "elite").

Like: a conversation filler that means nothing; example: "That test was like, really hard."

Lounge: the campus living space with dated furniture where you're supposed to "chill."

Manky: unappetizing or disgusting.

Meds: medicine for emotional needs; example: "He forgot to take his meds."

Mouse potato: someone who's addicted to the computer.

MPA: mysterious party accident; an inexplicable event that occurred while partying.

Munchapoloozas: consuming gross amounts of food.

Munchies: to engage in "munchapoloozas."

My bad: a way to apologize when it's your fault; example: "Hey, who finished the chips?" "Sorry, dude, my bad."

Natch: of course (from "naturally").

Parking Gestapo: police who hand out parking tickets.

Pizza pirating: conveniently forgetting to contribute toward the pizza.

Playing house: a couple who practically live together.

Pre-gaming: to party before a game.

Prep snooze: taking a nap to prep for a big night out.

Prozac shots: consuming cookie dough to lift your spirits.

Quack shack: college health facility.

Rents: parents; purse strings.

Sausage fest: a party where there are more guys than girls (see Antler festival).

Scamming: on the hunt for the opposite sex.

Schnoogle: an affectionate embrace.

Sco-Pro: scholastic probation.

Sexiled: being kicked out of your living space while your roommate has a "friend" over.

Shiny: good, awesome.

Snap!: an expression of affirmation or negation.

Sorostitute: a promiscuous female.

Tailgating: to party before a football game (also see Pre-gaming).

Throw me a bone: "Give me some help."

Trill: worthwhile, excellent.

Umpteen: infinite number.

Vanilla: very plain or having no excitement.

Waggle: to waste time.

Zombied: to stay up pulling an all-nighter.

Index

Grilled chicken sandwiches with sun-dried
tomatoes and goat cheese spread, 100
Grilled southwest chicken with black bean
salsa, 19
Old-fashioned chicken noodle soup, 33
Pasta alfredo with chicken, asparagus, and
tomatoes, 49
White chicken chili, 103

Chili. *See* Soups and chilis

Cookies and bars
Chocolate no-bake cookies, 26
Chocolate-orange squares, 91
Chocolate peanut butter balls, 59
Decadent chocolate brownies, 56
Dreamy lemon bars, 60
Old-fashioned granola bars, 55

Desserts
Apple cake with vanilla sauce, 58
Chocolate-dipped strawberries, 27
Chocolate no-bake cookies, 26
Chocolate-orange squares, 91
Chocolate peanut butter balls, 59
Decadent chocolate brownies, 56
Dreamy lemon bars, 60
Easy chocolate mousse, 89
Grandma's blueberry-apple crisp, 90
Key lime pie, 88

Mom's apple pie, 124
Old-fashioned granola bars, 55
Strawberry shortcakes, 28
Super-moist chocolate sheet cake, 120
White chocolate cheesecake, 122

Egg dishes
Easy quiche lorraine, 70
Eggs Benedict, 95
Homeboy egg and cheese muffins, 30
Spinach and mushroom frittata, 96

Fruit
Chocolate-dipped strawberries, 27
Cinnamon-maple apples, 31
Fruit and honey smoothies, 2
Healthy fruit salad, 9
Macadamia nut and banana pancakes with
caramel butter, 64
Strawberry shortcakes, 28

Mexican/Latino/Southwest
As you like it—Mexican salsa, 5
Authentic cheese enchiladas, 81
Chicken enchiladas in salsa verde, 107
Easy beef (or turkey) tacos, 15
Grilled southwest chicken with black bean
salsa, 19
Quesadillas with caramelized onions, 38
Southwest turkey burgers, 13